Praise for *Praying Circles around Your Marriage*

As they tell the story of their family's journey, Joel and Nina Schmidgall give an insider's view into the way they've drawn circles of prayer for their personal hopes and more. In the best times, those prayers have pushed them forward as a couple and as leaders. In the more difficult times, those prayers have been a backstop for a time of pause and reassessment. I've known them both for a very long time, and I know their commitment isn't limited to a prayer closet but compels them to the corridors of power and the streets of desperation. This book explains how.

Reggie and Debbie Joiner, founder and CEO of Orange

Michelle and I are so excited for *Praying Circles around Your Marriage,* and we can't wait for other couples to read this remarkable book. Pastor Joel and Nina Schmidgall have outlined how to create a joyful, prayerful fortress around your most important earthly relationship, keeping in and cultivating what is good and keeping out the things that harm. Their book will bless and inspire married couples, singles contemplating marriage, and pastors and leaders who work with couples. You don't want to miss this very special book!

Joshua and Michelle DuBois, executive director
of the White House Faith-based Initiative
under President Obama, CNN Commentator,
and CEO of Values Partnerships

Okay, true confession: I have a bias against marriage books because I think they make you feel guilty about yours. Good news: this is *not* that book. I am so glad Joel and Nina Schmidgall wrote this together. It's honest, real, challenging, practical, and vulnerable. It also points you to a surprising solution far too many people ignore—prayer. You'll love this book, and you'll love Joel and Nina.

Carey and Toni Nieuwhof, founding pastor of
Connexus Church and author of *Didn't See It Coming*

Your marriage will not only be strengthened, but you will experience great blessing if you practice daily prayer and Bible reading with your spouse.

Former Congressman Joseph R. Pitts, Pennsylvania

Joel and Nina Schmidgall have given us a profound gift—a handbook on prayer as the wellspring of biblical marriage. Engaged couples, newlyweds, and those, like us, who have passed the fifty-years-married mark need to read this book!

Dick and Ruth Foth, coauthors of *Known:*
Finding Deep Friendships in a Shallow World

Joel and Nina Schmidgall are two of our heroes in ministry and in marriage. Their commitment to their family and their calling is unmistakable, and they approach both with a sense of responsibility and a sense of humor. This book opens the curtain for the rest of us to learn how prayer is the bedrock of that commitment. We're excited to be able to read and apply these insights to our own marriage.

Geoff and Sherry Surratt, authors of *Together:*
A Guide for Couples in Ministry

Praying Circles
Around Your
Marriage

Praying Circles
Around Your
Marriage

Joel and Nina Schmidgall
with **Mark Batterson**

ZONDERVAN

Praying Circles around Your Marriage
Copyright © 2019 by Mark Batterson, Joel Schmidgall, Nina Schmidgall

Requests for information should be addressed to:
Zondervan, *3900 Sparks Dr. SE, Grand Rapids, Michigan 49546*

ISBN 978-0-310-35488-8 (hardcover)

ISBN 978-0-310-35493-2 (international trade paper edition)

ISBN 978-0-310-35492-5 (audio)

ISBN 978-0-310-35490-1 (ebook)

Authors are represented by the literary agency of The Fedd Agency, P.O. Box 341973, Austin, Texas 78734.

Cover design: Curt Diepenhorst
Interior design: Kait Lamphere

Printed in the United States of America

18 19 20 21 22 23 24 25 26 27 28 /LSC/ 15 14 13 12 11 10 9 8 7 6 5 4 3 2 1

To our church family, National Community Church,
and the couples who have given us the privilege of pastoring you.
Thank you for inviting us into your most sacred moments.

Contents

Foreword

About halfway into a message that Joel and Nina Schmidgall shared about marriage at National Community Church, we knew they needed to write the book you hold in your hands. As we listened, we realized how much we have to learn from them. The irony is that we've been married a decade longer than Joel and Nina! And Joel is Lora's younger brother! But their marriage is mature beyond its years. And we believe that God has graced them and called them to share those hard-earned lessons with you.

As family, we've witnessed every milestone in their marriage. We've shared lots of laughs and tears. And we've also had the joy of serving together at National Community Church. Joel serves as executive pastor and is the longest-tenured member of our staff, besides the two of us. When Nina started leading our kids ministry, NCC had a dozen kids on a good Sunday, including our three children. She now leads a team that serves hundreds of kids and youth, plus their parents, across our seven campuses. All of that to say this: we've been through the thick and thin of life and ministry together.

When Mark wrote *The Circle Maker*, we had no idea it would impact the prayer lives of millions of readers. And all the credit goes to God. He's the one who puts the right book in the right hands at the right time. That's the predominant prayer for every book Mark writes. And it's our prayer for this book as well. This book has the potential to change your marriage, even save your marriage. Well, not this book per se. More precisely, *prayer*!

Prayer is the difference between the best we can do and the best God can do. Prayer softens hearts, downloads wisdom, develops patience, exposes fear, challenges our thinking, and points us to the ultimate covenantal relationship with the One who loves us in the purest, most self-sacrificing way. When we grow in awareness of the Spirit who has been deposited in us, we find a deep well of resources to draw from. We would not be together twenty-six years later without submitting to the divine dance that must take place with a husband and wife and the Spirit of God. Love in true form is God, whether or not you realize it. But the voice of love can lose its volume over the years if we don't learn to tune back in.

Here's what we know for sure: Prayer is as important to marriage as anything you'll ever do. In *Praying Circles around Your Children*, Mark wrote, "You'll never be a perfect parent, but you can be a praying parent . . . Prayer turns ordinary parents into prophets who shape the destinies of their children."[1] What's true of parenting is true of marriage. You'll never be a perfect spouse, but you can be a praying spouse. There are moments in marriage when prayer is all you have left, but that doesn't mean it should be a last resort. If you prioritize prayer, it's preventative medicine.

Honestly, we wish we would've had this book when we got married. We did premarital counseling. We read some of the bestselling books at the time. But we got married so young that we had a lot of maturing to do as individuals and as a couple. Our first two years were the toughest years of our marriage because we had some growing up to do! Mark will often say, "We've been happily married for twenty-four years." After a pause, he'll add the punch line, "And we just celebrated our twenty-sixth anniversary." Do the math—our first two years were tough.

Part of the reason we like to share this is because not every marriage starts with a "honeymoon" phase. Don't get us wrong, we had some amazing moments and memories. But our early years involved more work than we originally imagined. We weren't as efficient as we could have been in the learning process because we tried to gut it out and figure it out by ourselves. We're so thankful for the Lord's grace on our marriage throughout the years and during some really tough seasons. If you're in one of those seasons, there is hope on the other side!

There are lots of people who have been following Christ for twenty-five years, but they don't have twenty-five years of experience. They have one year of experience repeated twenty-five times. Many marriages fall into the same trap. If we want our marriages to evolve, we've got to learn the lessons God is trying to teach us. We've had to learn a few lessons many times over! You don't have to be afraid of making mistakes. That's a given. But what we do with those mistakes, and whether we are willing to learn from them, will determine whether we grow closer or farther apart. Opening ourselves up to outside voices will sharpen the process, offer perspective, and set our course on a journey toward wholeness and oneness.

Like many couples, the two of us are very different from one another. Those differences can bring quite the adventure and perhaps some fireworks too. But the differences that often cause tension can become blessings in disguise if a couple can learn to complement one another. Each of us, and our differences, reflect different dimensions of God's character.

You can be selfish and married, but you cannot be selfish and happily married. Marriage is one way that God interrupts our preoccupation with ourselves. As you and your spouse work through this book, focus on meeting the needs of your spouse. If you focus on getting your needs met, you'll be swimming upstream against the current. There are two keys to changing the current: humility and prayer. We have a little mantra we say all the time: "If you stay humble and stay hungry, there's nothing God cannot do in you and through you!" That certainly applies to marriage. If you walk in Christlike humility and have a desire for oneness, you will gain wisdom and experience instead of repeating the same patterns. Humility is the key to unity. And prayer is the key to humility. It's a recognition that you cannot do this in your own strength, your own wisdom. Nothing has the potential to change relational momentum like prayer!

One last word of encouragement. When people are pursuing a dream, Mark will often remind them that it will take longer and be much harder than they originally imagined. But the payoff is always greater too. Marriage falls into that category. It is a God-ordained, God-sized dream. And no one said it would be easy. You wouldn't chase a career dream without a plan and some training and some determination, would you? Going after your marriage with the same kind of intensity is one of the best investments you can make. It's also one of the greatest gifts you can give your children.

In the pages that follow, Joel and Nina introduce seven circles. We love each one of them. And we have a hunch that two or three of those circles will hit you right where you are in your marriage. But stay tuned. If you pick this book back up in five years, it may hit a different nerve ending.

You will greatly benefit from this book if you read it individually, but may we also encourage you to consider reading this book with your spouse? In fact, why not read it with other couples? There will be paragraphs you'll need to process internally, but processing verbally with others can help catalyze change. Marriage is too often treated as a solo sport. Trust us when we say it's a team sport. And no one models that better than Joel and Nina. You'll read lots of stories about lots of marriages in this book, and that's because Joel and Nina have befriended and counseled lots of other couples. You'll also notice that they've learned from those couples as well.

As you read *Praying Circles around Your Marriage*, take time to stop and reflect. If a certain paragraph hits a nerve ending, talk about it and pray about it. You may even want to write notes in the margins. Mark likes to quote an old proverb: "The shortest pencil is longer than the longest memory." He won't even pick up a book if he doesn't have a pen in hand. Take time to underline the sentences that impact you and to jot down thoughts that jump out at you. And whatever you do, please follow the prayer prompts and practice the action prompts!

Enjoy the journey of praying circles around your marriage.

Mark and Lora Batterson

Circling Marriage

JOEL & NINA

*W*ith this ring, I thee wed."

It was a hot and sticky afternoon in August. The air was thick with humidity and the faces of our family and friends were flushed pink with heat. August is a prime month for weddings in Washington, D.C., but it is certainly not because the weather is pleasant. The United States Congress takes recess for the month, and the entire city takes a big, deep breath. Hardworking staff all over the city are able to take a much-needed vacation, with the result that many couples plan their nuptials during this time—and we were no exception.

Joel and I (Nina) had been planning the day for months, but nothing could have prepared us for the moment the church doors opened and I began to walk down the aisle. Joel stood at the end of the aisle flanked by his brother, Robb, and his brother-in-law, who is also our pastor, Mark Batterson.

Mark officiated the ceremony. I remember feeling so comforted to have these moments led by someone who knew and loved us so well. He told stories about us and gently reminded us of the depth of the commitment we were about to make. Finally we arrived at the moment we had been most anticipating: "Joel and Nina, turn and face one another."

Mark led us as we recited our vows to one another. The vows would be sealed with the exchange of rings. "This ring is a token of your undying love and your unending commitment to each other. Forsaking all others, do you promise to love and cherish Joel [to love and cherish Nina] as long as you both shall live?"

"I do," we said. And that was the day we stepped into the sacred circle of marriage.

A ring has been the symbol of a marriage covenant for generations. At its core, a ring is a circle. Because it has no beginning and no end, a circle represents the infinite. A circle represents the bold declaration of marriage. Exchanged during the wedding ceremony, the ring is an emblem of the sincerity and permanence of a couple's love for one another and regard for their marriage. A wedding ring is made of precious metals, purified by the heat of many fires. The center of a circle represents a door leading to known and unknown events: "for richer, for poorer, in sickness and in health." It is the symbol of destiny to pursue.

Circles are an ancient symbol of commitment without end, and to this day it remains deeply symbolic in a marriage ceremony. At traditional Jewish weddings there is a symbolic and intimate moment that is shared between bride and groom. As the bride proceeds down the aisle, she meets her groom under the *huppah* ("canopy"). Following her processional, the bride begins to circle the groom. Traditionally, the bride circles seven times. In more modern times, the ceremony has been adapted, with each partner circling the other three times and then the couple circling one final time together. The act of *hakafot*, the Hebrew word for "circling," is a deeply symbolic ritual. It represents compromise and unity within the sacred space of marriage. Seven is the number of completion and perfection in the Bible. This circling is a prayer and a declaration of partnership.

Prayer Revival

In *The Circle Maker*, Mark Batterson shared the legend from the Jewish Talmud of a man named Honi.[1] He was known as "the circle maker" because of his bold strategy of prayer. In a moment of deep need in the nation of Israel, he drew a circle around himself and publicly began to pray. His prayer was a declaration that he would not leave the circle until God blessed His people again. Honi's prayer was considered one of the most significant prayers in the history of Israel, the prayer that saved a generation.

We need this same bold resolve within marriages today. Marriages are suffering. Many couples are experiencing high levels of hurt and disappointment in their marriage. Young marriages are desperate for hope and direction to make their commitment last. Many single men and women are taking a look at the crumbling marriages of their parents and peers and wondering if the ring is even worth it.

We know it is a foundation of prayer that offers the hope in marriage. It is through prayer that challenges will be overcome, hurts will be healed, and commitments reestablished.

It is time for a prayer revival in our marriages.

We don't know the story of your marriage. But we know that God can strengthen it through prayer.

Marriage is a journey unique to each couple. Each couple will endure different story lines, some with more heartbreaks than others. Each individual enters marriage with different hang-ups, some more easy to overcome than others. Every marriage has different ailments. But there is one shared antidote: prayer.

You make just a few key decisions in life. You spend the rest of your life managing those decisions. Outside of a faith decision, marriage is the most important decision you will ever make. The greatest relationship decision deserves the greatest investment.

Through prayer, God can give you new eyes for your spouse. Through prayer, God can rekindle romance. Through prayer, God can align vision, overcome pain and resentment, and reenergize your friendship.

The richness of your marriage will be determined by how frequently and how fervently God is invited into your relationship. Prayer will draw you into unity with God and, as a result, with one another.

Marriage is the union of two imperfect people. Through prayer, you invite the presence of a perfect God.

In our roles at National Community Church, we've had the opportunity to be invited into many important ceremonies in the lives of individuals. None is more sacred than the ceremony to join two individuals in marriage.

Marriage is God's most sacred covenant. It was ordained by God to provide believers with a picture of Christ's love and relationship to His church. Ephesians 5:32 calls marriage "a profound mystery." It is pointing to something bigger, revealing the day when we will become one with Christ. It is our great privilege to walk with couples as they step into this important relationship.

We see the real-life struggles of couples as they do the hard work of merging two lives. There is sometimes pain; often there's misunderstanding. It always requires perseverance.

Not only have we been invited to come alongside couple to prepare for marriage and to officiate their wedding ceremony, but we have been invited into the sacred space of marriages when a couple faces hurdles or needs support. Couples graciously open their lives and allow us to walk with them and support them in prayer and counsel. It is some of the most important work we do.

Our own road to marriage was not an easy one. We are as different as two people can be. We come from different backgrounds and engage with the world from very different experiences. In fact, sometimes we marvel at the oddity of our partnership.

Opposites Attract

If you are familiar with various personality tests, you will understand just how different we are from each one another. We have the exact opposite Myers-Briggs personality makeup. All four letters. We do not share any of the same "strengths" on the Gallup Strengths Finder assessment. Nope, not one. We are different Enneagram numbers. We have reverse order of results on the spiritual gifts assessment. Yes, we are that different.

- When driving somewhere, Nina prefers directions to come in a step-by-step list. Joel never hits Start on the app for the map on his phone; he just looks at the overall picture of a map, zooming in to figure out the necessary turns.

- Nina is animated and assertive. Joel is relaxed and flexible.
- Nina says a lot of words. Joel says less. Joel will tell people he is the headlines and Nina is the fine print.
- Nina's love languages are acts of service and verbal affirmation. Joel's is . . . food.
- When enjoying a meal, Nina prefers to share food and experience a meal together. Joel, very much, does not. Your food. My food. The end.
- While sleeping, Nina likes three blankets on. Joel likes three fans on.

These differences are not limited to just our preferences. We think differently from one another. We navigate conflict differently. We have different response tendencies. We see the world through different lenses, do not make decisions in the same way, and are motivated by different things.

While this has potential to create a beautiful and powerful complement to one another, it also has potential for conflict and misunderstanding. It requires a lot of hard work and commitment to stay unified and connected. It takes prayers for insight and understanding.

As we walk together, let us share a little more about who we are. Our marriage is made up of two very flawed people. We are best friends, and our marriage is filled with love and laughter. (We got an extra dose of silly that we are trying desperately to pass along to our kids!) However, our marriage takes work every day, and it wasn't an easy road to fuse our very different lives.

Our Story

NINA

My desire for marriage and family was placed in my heart at a very young age, even before I knew the Lord. I didn't grow up in a home of faith and didn't come to understand Jesus as the hero in my story until middle school.

My parents were young loves who married very young, had me right away, and divorced while I was still a baby. I am from a blended family—one that had been blended and squished and stretched a number of times over.

Even in the midst of broken marriages around me, I had a desire for marriage and motherhood from as early as I can remember. Recently, I found a journal that was a student assignment in the third grade. In a poem called "Someday," I wrote a list of hopes and dreams for my future. There at the bottom, just under my plan to visit Japan, my eight-year-old self declared, "Someday I will be married, and a happy marridge [that's how I spelled it back then] that will be."

My journals throughout adolescence and into adulthood echoed my desire to have a healthy, strong, and lifelong marriage. When I met the Lord and came to understand how marriage was a picture of His relationship to His church, it gave a greater understanding to my longings.

Like many kids from blended or broken homes, I was left trapped between desperate longings for marriage and terrible fears about it as well. I carried a lot of reservations about my ability to find success in lifelong marriage.

As I grew into adulthood and began to experience some

bumps and hiccups in my own dating life, I had to confront some deep fears about whether I even knew how to have a healthy relationship or had any of the tools to have the marriage I desired. Most of my fears were rooted in my own concerns about my inadequacies, and every failure I had in relationships validated those concerns.

I met Joel my very first night in Washington, D.C. I had just moved to town, and a friend invited me to dinner at the house where Joel also lived. He was tall, confident, and so funny, and I was smitten as soon as I met him. I resolved to keep showing up in his path, visiting the church where he worked and going to events I hoped he was attending. It was a year before Joel asked me out on our first date.

Our relationship grew slowly. While it's true that opposites attract, we had a lot of work to do to come to an understanding of one another and to make our backgrounds and personalities come into alignment. Of course, dating years kick up all the issues you don't necessarily realize are at work in the subnarrative of your life.

I wondered whether I could trust someone to commit to me, despite my flaws and weaknesses. Joel seemed very alarmed about any conflict we might encounter, and it made him hesitant to enter into marriage. His hesitations only fueled my self-doubt.

I struggled with how much time and work it took to come to a place where we could consider marriage. At the time, I couldn't see the healing process the Lord was doing in me through our relationship.

So many young people are looking for marriage to be the answer to wounds or gaps in their lives. Marriage doesn't complete you, but, in fact, it exposes you. It exposes sin and weakness and can open the door for either healing or further damage.

While I didn't see it at the time, the Lord knew exactly what I needed in order to have the marriage I had hoped and prayed for. He had plans to use it as a refining tool to shape and grow me.

The Lord knew I needed someone unwavering. Joel is deliberative and hesitant when it comes to decisions. But he is resolute and unwavering in every commitment he makes. For someone who grew up with fears about instability, Joel has provided stability.

The things that are difficult in the dating years are usually there to stay. But through growth and persistent prayer, they can be the very things that aid in overcoming. Imperfect but just right, our story is one for which I am so grateful.

JOEL

Growing up, I had a genuine appreciation for my parents' marriage. They were a team, seemed to never fight, and loved us kids. I thought marriage should be effortless. I realize now that was a naive idea. But I also later realized I had developed unrealistic and unhealthy expectations. As I understood it, to argue meant incompatibility. If you had to work through issues, it meant you *had* issues. I thought a relationship shouldn't have any. I came to realize that my parents had done such a good job of sheltering us from their challenges, fights, and incompatibilities that I didn't know how to work through those things myself.

My dad was an influential man who held things close to the

vest. My mom is a sweet and kind woman who goes with the flow. What appeared to be compatibility and agreement actually had layers of conversations and prayer when the children weren't around. As kids, we saw the output, not the input. I had a lot to learn. I thought perfection was the only option, but I fell far short of it. And I held high expectations for any future partner.

In the beginning of my young adult years, I entered a dating relationship that grew serious. I had found someone who knew me like no one else, and someone I thought I knew more than anyone else. My parents shared with me some concerns about the relationship, but I wouldn't hear it. After four years, the relationship came to a sudden and devastating end. Learning the extent of the deception, I found myself in shock. Honestly, it messed me up. The devastating end to that relationship was magnified when I lost my dad suddenly to a heart attack soon after. It was the darkest season of my life. My brain was a fog; my heart had trouble finding hope; and I developed skepticism toward marriage. As I often do, I pushed all of those feelings underneath the surface.

But a truly authentic and connected relationship doesn't allow you to live on the surface. If I were ever to marry, I had to learn how to let someone else in. Through prayer, I asked God to do a healing work in me and allow me to build trust again.

I had already been living and working in Washington, D.C., for a few years before I met Nina. She was invited to dinner in the house where I lived with a bunch of guys. Goodness gracious! She was out of my league. She was gorgeous, smart, fun—a young up-and-comer on Capitol Hill. I was immediately attracted to her and her magnetic personality.

What I didn't realize was that Nina would be the one to draw out all the good, the bad, and the hidden in me. I had been in enjoyable relationships, but Nina really made me a better person. Sometimes it was through inspiration and sometimes through confrontation. Revelations came through Nina, and I was forced to draw them out through prayer. As I committed to be vulnerable and open with Nina, God was faithful to do a work in me that I couldn't do myself.

The Marriage Commitment

We both love attending weddings, but Nina *really* loves them. Well, Nina loves any party-like atmosphere but weddings include so many of Nina's favorite things—like family and friends and dancing and romance and eternal declarations of love . . . and, of course, good food! Lately, many bride and grooms are getting cute with their wedding vows. Like, "I commit to watching movies other than romantic comedies. And I promise always to root for the Chicago Cubs!" Well, that is what Joel would have asked to include if we had gotten cute with our vows. Except Joel would have also added a commitment to nightly foot rubs and going out to eat Ethiopian food regularly.

The delivery of the vows is usually an epic moment, a profession of love and admiration. But the truth is that a *vow* made before God and community is so much more than a declaration of *present* love; it's a mutually binding promise of *future* love.

A marriage vow is not a one-time commitment and it's covered for life. It is an everyday commitment. It is a commitment to daily lay down one's own needs and desires.

The Bible offers us a picture of marriage as a reflection of Christ's relationship with His church. But we live in a culture where the presentation of marriage has been grossly distorted. Our culture convinces us that marriage is something *for* me rather than something asked *of* me.

The love required in marriage is the love that calls us to submit to one another, to love like Christ loved the church. The entire New Testament clarifies that the kind of love Jesus showed is a sacrificial love. Philippians 2 describes Christ as emptying Himself and taking on the form of a servant.

Conversations with people who want to be married sometimes reveal that they are often more focused on what they'll get rather than what they'll be required to give.

Marriage does have many incredible blessings. Both of us would confess that our marriage is *the* greatest gift the Lord has given each of us. But let us be very clear that it is hard! To keep it healthy and strong, it is also the single biggest commitment the Lord has ever asked of us.

The call to deny oneself on behalf of another is the highest sacrifice either of us have been asked to make.

When the Bible speaks of love, it is measured not in how much you want to receive but in how much you are willing to give of yourself.

On our wedding day, before he led us to recite our vows, Mark's message reminded us that in marriage, we have to "yield the right of way" to one another day after day. That's the way he described the mutual submission into which we were stepping.

When you dreamed of marriage, what were you imagining? Is that the way you are living today?

Prayer Partnership:
Mark and Lora Batterson

The story of the circle maker has changed millions of lives since Mark wrote it. We don't take lightly the honor it is to be asked by Mark and Lora to write this book. We are grateful to be entrusted with inviting the miraculous work of prayer into the sacred covenant of marriage.

We've had the great privilege of serving alongside Mark and Lora at National Community Church since its earliest days. Together in ministry, we have walked through victories and heartaches, shared countless laughs and memories, and endured innumerable stresses. They have invited us into a beautiful partnership in ministry and also opened their lives to us. Just ahead of us in marriage, ministry, and parenting, they have been our biggest cheerleaders and the greatest investors in our family.

There isn't much we can share about marriage that doesn't have their fingerprints of influence. Mark and Lora have never held anything back from us, sharing transparently about the struggles and joys in marriage. It is from their marriage that we've learned how to show appreciation and support for one another. They have shown us an example of commitment to family above everything else. By modeling deep and sacrificial generosity, Mark and Lora have taught us what it looks like to build a marriage that can be used powerfully for the kingdom.

Above all, Mark and Lora have modeled a marriage built on a deep and consistent prayer life. They circle each other, their children, their family, their church. They pray bold and consistent prayers.

Lora and Joel, brother and sister, were raised in a legacy of prayer. The dedication in *The Circle Maker* is written to Mark's father-in-law, Joel and Lora's dad: "To my father-in-law, Bob Schmidgall. The memory of you kneeling in prayer lives forever, as do your prayers."[2]

It is this legacy of prayer on which both the Batterson and Schmidgall marriages stand. Through prayer, the Lord is invited to take the lead in our lives every day.

Evaluated Experience: The Toyota Way

Much has been written about the Toyota Production System (TPS) known for reforming the automotive manufacturing industry. "The Toyota Way" is a commitment to ensuring high quality at the lowest cost while minimizing waste.

After World War II, the Japanese economy was absolutely devastated, and a textile-company-turned-automobile-manufacturer was on the brink of bankruptcy. Its debt was eight times its capital value. More than seventy years later, Toyota is valued at thirty trillion yen. So, what in the world happened? The short answer is kaizen. Kaizen is a manufacturing process that focuses on small incremental adjustments to ensure continuous improvement.

Eiji Toyoda was a Japanese industrialist and one of the founders of the Toyota Motor Corporation. In 1950, Toyoda took a team of engineers on a twelve-week study tour of automobile plants in the United States. The Toyota Corporation was producing about nine hundred vehicles per month, one-tenth of what Ford was producing. They expected to be amazed, but it was quite the opposite. They were surprised by the inefficiencies in

American assembly lines. They actually saw an opportunity to catch up, and they have. In 2017, Toyota had a 15 percent market share, second only to General Motors. They now compete neck and neck with Ford.

Toyota's success rests on those small, continuous improvements. In fact, Toyota invests a million dollars every hour in research and development. Maybe that's why 80 percent of Toyotas purchased twenty years ago are still on the road today! That's a remarkable shelf life. It traces back to a reconnaissance trip in 1950, coupled with kaizen. It's the Toyota Way.

What if men and women took a similar "study tour" of their marriage? Can you imagine what we might learn about each other—what works well and what doesn't, our strong points as well as our shortcomings? Sadly, many couples don't really take an evaluated look at their marriage. All too often, couples put their most precious relationship on automatic pilot and wonder why it suffers. There are a few lessons we can learn from Toyota.

The Toyota Way starts with new employees standing in a circle drawn in chalk on the factory floor. Their first task? To stand in the circle and observe everything that's happening. The new employee is told to observe and take note of what they see. That's no easy job because there are lots of moving pieces to the process of building a car. Similarly, marriage also has lots of moving pieces. There's much to observe and note.

In this book, we will encourage you on a journey to improve your marriage. As we begin, we invite you to step into the marriage circle. Look long and hard.

The Toyota executives understand that the key to growth isn't experience; it's *evaluated* experience.

Prayer is the best evaluator. Honest conversation with God about your marriage will give you the greatest insight for innovation, conviction, and hope. As you read this book, we hope you will get in the circle and take a look around.

We want to encourage you to begin to build a legacy of prayer within your own marriage. In the seven chapters that follow, we'll invite you to circle different areas of your marriage. Note that each of us has written alternating chapters. To make it clear, we've noted at the beginning of the chapter which one of us is writing.

- **Vision Circle** (Joel): How to combine two unique visions for a new and combined purpose together.
- **War Circle** (Nina): How to understand the roots of conflict and see it as an opportunity for growth and greater connection.
- **Romance Circle** (Joel): How to avoid the transactional and cultivate a connected and intimate relationship.
- **Dance Circle** (Joel): How to merge interests, personalities, and histories as a partnership, fluid in movement and motion. How to posture to serve your spouse and position him/her to be used greatly.
- **Support Circle** (Nina): How to surround your marriage with a healthy support community that will offer encouragement, inspiration, perspective, support, and accountability.
- **Storm Circle** (Nina): How to build a foundation for your marriage that will help you weather the trials that are sure to come.
- **Legacy Circle** (Joel): How to leverage your marriage to have influence for generations.

We hope you will read this book with your spouse. Your investment can start as you read together. Throughout the book, we have included places that prompt you to prayer and to action. We encourage you to seriously consider the prompts and pause to pray as you read. Consider stopping to journal your prayers or take note of things the Lord speaks to you.

You can overcome the distance in your marriage through prayer.

The dreams you hope to realize in your family can be achieved through prayer.

The challenges facing your family can be overcome through prayer.

What your marriage will become is determined by how you pray. Prayers for your marriage will allow you to claim God-given promises, fulfill God-given dreams for your family, and seize a God-ordained legacy for generations.

You can have a peace-filled home. You can have companionship. You can achieve dreams. You can have understanding, unity, joy.

Prayer is the secret weapon.

Let's start circling.

Chapter 1

Vision Circle

JOEL

O K Houston, we've had a problem here."[1]
On April 13, 1970, at 9:09 p.m., disaster struck when the spacecraft Odyssey carrying the Apollo 13 crew was shaken by an onboard explosion. The Apollo 13 mission was intended to be the third manned lunar landing. Astronauts Jim Lovell, Jack Swigert, and Fred Haise had left earth two days before, en route to the moon.

A routine maintenance check of the systems resulted in an explosion of one of the spacecraft's oxygen tanks. Suddenly, the lives of the astronauts were at risk. The command module's normal supply of electricity, light, oxygen, and water was lost. There was just one small problem. They were 200,000 miles from earth.

Over the coming hours, the crew scrambled to come up with emergency procedures to return the astronauts safely home.

The astronauts and NASA's Mission Control Center were faced with enormous logistical problems in stabilizing the spacecraft and its air supply and ensuring successful reentry into earth's atmosphere.

Navigation was another problem, and Apollo 13's course had to be repeatedly corrected. Without power to the ship's computers, all navigation and targeting functions were unavailable. The explosion had created a cloud of debris around the spacecraft that inhibited visibility. The crew couldn't discern the stars from the particles glimmering in the light from the sun.

Without vision, the crew could not successfully navigate the incredible challenges facing them. Without the ability to use the stars to orient themselves, the astronauts could not set themselves on a course to safety.

Marriage starts out with grand vision—a shared way of seeing what you hope your future together will be. It is exciting and full of possibilities. But for many, marriage becomes filled with problems we never anticipated and for which we do not have the tools to navigate. Unanticipated problems throw us off course, and we don't know how to reorient. Some couples lose sight of their destination, while others never had a clear vision in the first place.

What is the vision for your marriage? Have you ever paused to figure out the direction your marriage is headed? If not, how will you reorient if you get thrown off course? When disaster strikes and you lose visibility, how will you reorient to redirect the ship?

At the height of racial tensions in the 1960s, Martin Luther King Jr. prophetically wrote from prison of the church's problem and responsibility in the division of people. He called the church to not just be a taillight, shining a light on what went wrong, but to be a headlight, shining a light on what could be.

Most of us can give a detailed explanation of the problems in our marriage. We can tell you every selfish, frustrating, and just plain annoying thing the other person does. But it is not the ability to identify problems that will lead to wholeness; it is our commitment to shine a light on what could be that will bring solutions.

If you're like most couples, it's all too easy to let the throes of everyday life take priority away from cultivating a larger purpose that will unify you even in the most turbulent times.

Through almost twenty years of pastoral work at a church made up primarily of individuals in their twenties and thirties, we've been able to counsel numerous couples. Many of them struggle with aligning individual visions that compete with one another. They can find themselves in a tug-of-war in pursuit of personal calling.

We see this magnified in Washington, D.C. Talented and passionate young people move to this city to pursue long-held dreams. Many find equally gifted partners and decide to marry. They quickly find it isn't easy to merge two passionate and competing visions, and they begin to pull against one another. If either spouse has had to give up more than the other, resentment can build and unity can begin to dissolve.

A couple very close to us had to work through something like this. Dave and Kate are two of the most gifted individuals you'll ever meet. Both of them are smart, passionate, and entrepreneurial. They are compassionate and thoughtful, and both are well read and incredibly articulate.

When Kate was just a teenager, God gave her a vision for telling the stories of the work He was doing around the world.

Listening to a missionary who had flown home to share about their work to their church, Kate shares, "I felt such an injustice that this missionary had come so far to give such a subpar presentation of what was clearly powerful, wonderful work that God was doing. I had this conviction that there had to be a better way to tell the story of what God is doing in the world."

As soon as Dave and Kate were married, they moved to Scotland to support a church plant while Dave got his master's degree in peacebuilding. At the end of the term, they returned to the United States, and Dave successfully pursued a number of different things like pastoring and filmmaking, but he couldn't get clarity on God's specific direction.

When Dave and Kate returned home to the United States, Kate decided to launch the dream that God had put on her heart at such a young age. On her twenty-sixth birthday, she walked into an office in downtown D.C. to register her new company, Bittersweet Creative.[2] Bittersweet would be a creative company that would produce a magazine to tell the stories of organizations that do inspiring work all around the world in response to the critical social issues of our day. Bittersweet would use print and film to tell the stories of hope and inspiration.

As Kate's passion began to become a reality, Dave wrestled for clarity for his purpose. He shares in retrospect that it was deeply unsettling to feel a prompt for larger things but not to get clarity on exactly what that might be. Kate's developing success began to affect Dave's level of security and made it difficult for him to support her well. They went through a season that felt more like a competition, and it began to put pressure on their marriage.

Since their earliest days of dating, both Dave and Kate had

a sense that their relationship was about something bigger than both of them. They knew their relationship was supposed to be outwardly focused on others, but the individual pursuit, pride, and jealousy were pulling them apart.

What we have found with many couples we counsel who start to feel this tension is that they can do the hard work of gaining consensus about merging their lives—and then circumstances change and the scales tip. Each time a season changes, a couple can find themselves having to renegotiate the terms. New challenges emerge that put new pressure on the relationship. An educational or vocational opportunity presents itself to one partner. The couple unexpectedly encounters a family or health crisis. A couple decides to relocate and must navigate new relationships and environments. In the midst of all of these changes, if the couple is not careful, the relationship can be reduced to a scoreboard or a scale that measures who is bending the most.

As vocations change, as kids enter the picture, as life changes course in a variety of ways, a shared vision can help a couple stay centered on what matters most. Without vision, we're left to survival mode. But with vision, we walk in purpose.

PRAYER PROMPT: Maybe you find yourself in one of these seasons right now. Maybe you feel like the terms of your relationship have changed and you're having to give more than what feels fair. Ask God to remind you of a larger purpose for your marriage. Ask Him to reveal how He plans to use you.

Schmidgall Core Values

Early on in our marriage, we seemed to have repetitive and recycled conflict. We were two active individuals trying to merge our lives. Nina would often work until very late at night, staying to help members of Congress through late-night votes. I was in the early years of helping lead an upstart growing church. Our small staff meant we were all involved day or night, weekday or weekend.

We were each trying to pursue our personal goals and trying to find time to forge this new priority of marriage. This meant a lot of unmet expectations. In the newer days of a relationship, it can feel like every conflict waged is somehow establishing boundaries that will play out for the rest of your marriage. You don't want to give up territory you may never get back. Marriage feels a little bit like *Risk*, the board game of global domination. "I can't surrender South America to you. I'll never get it back!" In our case, we tended to focus on what each one of us was giving up instead of focusing on what we were forging together. To do so is a recipe for a lot of arguments!

We needed a vision. A *vision*, a shared way of seeing, begets a clarifying *purpose*, a shared way of doing, that helps us navigate decisions. We had to step out of our individualistic approach and grip a vision from God for us. We had to die to self and stop trying to establish our own ways.

I thought mature love would be achieved when we stopped arguing so much. But what I've realized is that mature love is more about the pursuit of purpose. We will never have an argument-less marriage. But I do know that when we're focused on a sense of *calling*, the arguments lose steam and intensity and seem to become inconsequential. A healthy, connected marriage is not about the absence of conflict as much as about the presence of purpose.

How did we arrive at a place of shared vision?

In those hard years at the beginning of marriage, Nina and I really wrestled in prayer over what we wanted to be about and how we wanted to organize our lives. It turned out that those conflicts about how to spend our time were not in vain. As we did the hard work to hash out our different priorities, shared commitments started to rise to the surface. Over the years, we began to ask ourselves hard questions.

- What sort of impact do we want to make on our community?
- What do we care about that we can both rally around?
- What set of gifts are unique to us as a couple?
- Where do we work best together?

Through diligent prayer, especially when we did not feel like we were on the same page, God began to reveal some things. We mined our histories and evaluated where our relationship brought life to us and to others. We asked God for discernment about how to be obedient to Jesus' words and how to honor the way He had created each of us. Certain themes began to show themselves. Finally we wrote them into a list of core values: **service**, **adventure**, **generosity**, **courage**, and **honor**. We wanted these words to direct us, to motivate us, to remind us of our priorities.

As we started to identify our values, a unified vision started to become clearer. We wrapped these values into a simple mantra that is found in Acts 20:35. We want to *give more than we receive*. The *vision* birthed from those *values* helped us walk in *purpose*.

Values → Vision → Purpose

In other words, we start with what's important to us—our values. These values shape what we hope for in the future—our vision. And finally, this shared way of seeing turns into a shared way of living—our purpose.

The simple mantra was a statement that gave us direction as a couple. Early in our marriage, it meant we used our house to host others, even if it was inconvenient. We had guests so often that we called our home "Hotel Schmidgall." It meant making sacrifices in our budget so we could give regularly to missions or make a gift to the DC Dream Center, a mentoring project we support.[3] Over the years it has meant making the time to go to the performance or sporting event of a young person in our life or putting aside work emails at night to drop off hot chocolate and snacks to the friends experiencing homelessness in our neighborhood. We found ourselves saying a more unified yes to opportunities that fit with a vision that God had birthed in us together. It has meant remaining committed to meeting needs in ways that don't necessarily benefit us.

We have come back to this simple statement of vision thousands of times. We whisper it to each other in decision moments. We encourage each other with it in times of discouragement. We have found that it doesn't just give us a path to dream about our calling; it also gives perspective to our problems and purpose to our pain.

Vision will do that. It leads you in purposeful living. It gives you resolve when you are tired. It gives you determination in the difficult. Amazingly, it can bring retroactive joy to the pain of the past. Why do you think we sing songs in church about the cross? The cross was an instrument of torture and pain. It was an act of brutality. Yet we sing about the wonderful cross with such joy. Why? It is because of the incredible purpose that came out of that pain—a purpose so deep that it not only gives us joy today but allows us to reach back and celebrate those moments of deep pain for Christ. A vision is a gift that will absolutely change your past perspective and reorder your future conversations and actions.

When marriage gets tough, many couples want to bow out. Sometimes couples will call for the lifeboat before the vision has even been revealed. It is through the hardest moments that revelation often comes. This is where the commitment sustains.

Vision Begins with Covenant

The birth of vision begins in the deepest level of commitment—a covenant. The Hebrew word for "covenant" is the word *berith*. It's used 280 times in the Old Testament and is derived from a root that means "to cut." It's a reference to ancient covenant making, where an animal was divided into two parts, and the covenanting parties passed between the two parts. They were essentially saying, "If we don't abide by this covenant, may we end up like the animal that was cut in two." But whether a business relationship, a marriage relationship, or any covenant relationship during that time, there were consequences for breaking covenant.

What if that had been a part of your marriage ceremony?

Cue "Canon in D." The doors swing open for father and daughter in white wedding gown. The audience stands and smiles and begins to takes photos of this beautiful bride . . . walking between a sliced heifer. Hello!

It is interesting to note that the tradition of family and friends of the bride and groom sitting on the opposite side of the aisle from each other was to symbolize this cutting of the covenant. The white runner down the center aisle is placed as holy ground for the bride and groom to meet in the middle, representing their covenant commitment. So, the meaning is not completely lost in our tradition.

But historically, for the covenant to come to life, there had to be a death. To grasp a vision from God for our marriage, it doesn't start by asking what I want out of marriage. Getting a vision for your marriage starts by dying to self and surrendering to God. Marriage is God's assault and attack on my selfishness and His rebirth in me of selflessness. That doesn't happen in a moment, but in every moment of marriage.

Though a couple stands in front of the officiant to give their vows, the covenant they are making is not made to the person officiating the wedding or even to the guests. It is a covenant made to God. In the same way, a vision for a marriage will come only from God—not from any other source.

Through prayer, God will reveal His vision for your marriage. Begin by surrendering your marriage to God. Let go of your pride, your wants, your personal pursuits. Ask God in prayer to make His wants and vision your wants and vision. Seek to find out who God has made you to be as a couple and why He has brought you together.

ACTION PROMPT: Stop here and begin to surrender your marriage to God. Ask God to help you let go of your personal agenda and to reveal why He has brought you and your spouse together. Can you reduce it to a sentence or a list of values?

Unique Imprint

Fingerprints are one of those physical attributes that help us understand that each person is created entirely unique. The tiny ridges, whorls, and valley patterns on a person's finger are entirely unique to that person. In fact, no two fingerprints have ever been found alike in billions of comparisons.

Just as each of us has a unique fingerprint, each of us also has a persona that is entirely individual and unduplicated. Made up of our differing personalities and perspectives, intertwined with our different life experiences and circumstances, this means every person is entirely unique and will have a unique imprint on the world.

Mark Batterson calls this a person's "soulprint," and in his book by the same name, he writes, "There has never been and never will be anyone else like you. But that isn't a testament to you. It's a testament to the God who created you."[4]

Before a couple gets married, they exist as two separate individuals. Each individual has a unique history, gift set, interests, and vision for their future. And when two people come together in marriage, you create a unique marriage print.

Your marriage has an identity that cannot be replicated by any other couple. Together you and your spouse can impact others in a way no other couple can. Let's look at the ways these circles come together, which illustrate different approaches to marriage.

Attachment

In this approach to marriage, we find a spouse to do life alongside. Often when a person thinks about marriage, they are considering whose circle they might want to attach their circle to. In this situation, a spouse doesn't take away from who you are, but they are going to come alongside you, supporting your vision and pursuing their own vision as well. It's a mutually beneficial marriage. The common vision is individuals who care for and support the other.

In his assessment of marriage and community in Jewish tradition, Rabbi Maurice Lamm points to Rabbi Joseph Soloveitchik's description of how Jewish philosopher Maimonides distinguished the different approaches to friendship within marriage. The attachment approach is called *haver le'davar*.[5] It is a utilitarian association that depends on whether or not each person is useful to the other. When the usefulness disappears, "the bond of love disappears."[6]

Too often a person will attach their individual circle to another but refrain from making any real sacrifices of their personal goals or agenda. This loose sort of attachment makes it very easy to break the two circles apart again should the relationship no longer be beneficial to either party.

Alignment

In this picture of marriage, one person comes together with another, and they intentionally try to merge parts of their lives. The Jewish term *haver le'daagah* speaks of having a person with whom one can share troubles, sorrows, and joys, which will lighten the load for each. As Rabbi Lamm writes, "Joys are multiplied and sorrows are divided when they are shared."[7]

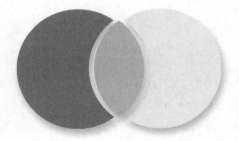

In this approach, each person maintains his or her own dreams, ideas, and work. But they have combined ideas and relationships. In its ideal, this approach protects individualism while also being intentional about combining life in certain areas. The common vision is found in whatever areas the couple shares in common.

Marriage Print

In this approach to marriage, we find a picture of oneness. Each individual will always maintain the uniqueness of who God has made them to be individually—their history, personality, and image. But every part of the person has an influence on the larger vision of the couple as a whole.

When you draw the circle around the entirety of who you are together in marriage, you are still one, but God expands and multiplies your vision. This approach releases the focus on self. It paints a picture that marriage requires all of you but produces more than the both of you. Recognizing the larger circle as a vision granted from the Lord, this approach focuses less on individual benefit and more on kingdom purpose.

For this approach, the Jewish term *haver le'deah* applies— "a joint dedication to common goals." It is a "dream of realizing great ideals, with a readiness to sacrifice to achieve for their attainment."[8]

This is what we refer to as your marriage print. It is the joint dedication to a greater vision—a vision that is realized through your marriage in a greater way than it could be realized individually. By identifying your unique marriage print and determining how to lean in and maximize it, you can leverage your marriage for meaning and impact.

The couple we mentioned before, Dave and Kate, who were feeling divided in their individual pursuits, now have one of the most beautiful examples of a marriage print. While each of their individual careers had really started to take off, Dave and Kate felt like they were pulling against one another rather than sharing a unified vision. Uncomfortable with the way their pursuits were distancing them from each other, they began to pray that God would align their visions.

A number of years into their marriage, Dave began a forty-day prayer challenge with a group of guys. The Lord began to do such a powerful work in each of the men that they decided to extend it to a full year. Prompted by the promises in 2 Chronicles 7:14, they prayed together every morning at 7:14 a.m. Dave considers the revelations through prayer that year to be the turning point for revealing a vision for their marriage.

Dave explains, "Something deepened in my heart for Kate during that year of prayer. I started to increase my prayers, and it began to deepen my own convictions. God began to dethrone our own ambitions so we could genuinely honor what God has put in each other." They committed to embrace and champion each other's pursuits. They began to claim each other's victories as their own.

God began to reveal a shared vision. Through prayer, they

asked God for clarity about the "culture" of their marriage. He gave them His word in Isaiah 58:12—that they would be "Repairer of Broken Walls, Restorer of Streets with Dwellings." This led them to focus on people and places of conflict. As a couple, they jointly committed to seek the kingdom here on earth now.

Just as that important year of prayer was coming to a close, God gave them an opportunity to buy a sizable home in D.C. that would become a hub for the work they do together. It is a place of reconciliation where people of all backgrounds and positions can be brought together. They house refugees, feed and entertain marginalized neighborhood youth, and host opportunities for learning and connection.

Kate continues to lead Bittersweet, telling the story of hope and inspiration amid poverty, corruption, disease, devastation, and abuse. Dave serves as a pastor, doing peacemaking work in the diverse communities of Washington, D.C. Dave says, "It's been an evolution of two very different visions that have remained unique but are now somehow beautifully working together. While we are still two unique seeds, we finally feel planted in the same soil."

The couples we see with the deepest connection and greatest unity are the ones who, like Dave and Kate, have sought the Lord for a revelation of shared vision.

Shared Vision: The Antidote to a Thousand Arguments

The reason that businesses create policies and procedures is to be able to make a thousand decisions at one time. Otherwise, they have to make a decision about each new circumstance, each new day. In many ways, clarifying vision is doing the same thing in your relationship. There is power in predecision to guide priorities.

The word *division* is made up of two parts. The prefix *di* means "two." So the word *division* means "two visions." The reason so many marriages live in constant conflict is that there are two visions in the home.

Do you have a vision in your marriage or do you have di-vision?

Luke 11:17 tells us, "Any kingdom divided against itself will be ruined, and a house divided against itself will fall."

Most couples have not consciously thought about this, but there's great hope for your future if you can start here and now. If you continue to coexist with two visions, your house will reap what you sow. But when you buy in to a shared vision, it is like predeciding a thousand decisions before they are ever made.

One way this plays out for Nina and me is in the way we manage our finances. We have already predecided to do our best to live a life of service and sacrifice. We seek to give more than we receive. While this includes our time, it also has financial implications. This means we don't have to have a conversation every month about whether we will tithe or give to missions organizations. We have already made those predecisions before any money hits our bank account. This helps us avoid the tendency to overspend or just serve ourselves. When we take a look at our calendar for the month, we are able to avoid many disagreements when we let our values guide our decisions. We have guidelines in place that help us ensure that our priorities are driving our commitments.

Vision Directs

In an age in which we use our electronic devices to direct us, it is hard to remember the long, painstaking path that navigators took to help people find their way. Historically, navigation has included dependence on constant objects of the physical world— the sun, the moon, the stars—and using them to find one's way in the world. For thousands of years, navigators, sailors, and astronomers used the North Star, also known as Polaris, as their true north, relying on it to give them a sense of direction. The North Star lies nearly in a direct line with the axis of the earth's rotation, making it appear motionless in the sky. This makes it an excellent fixed point to use for navigation.

Vision gives us a sense of our true north. It won't mean that every decision will be based on a predetermined standard. It just serves as a marker to direct or redirect our path and ensure we're staying true to our desired course.

In our case, our shared vision helps push those 55/45 decisions in a certain direction. It holds us accountable to make sure that as a whole, we're always finding ways to allow our marriage to bless outwardly. We don't use shared vision to force our way. Shared vision is not a rule to follow; it's a North Star that guides.

Vision Source

You may have a strong sense that there is a purpose for your marriage, but it hasn't been revealed to you yet. Just like the mountains hidden in the night, you know God's vision is there, but you just can't see it yet. You want to know how to get a clear revelation of that vision.

I have a strong memory of the first time my family took a

vacation outside of the Chicago area. We arrived in Colorado late at night and drove to our little cabin in a small town called Frisco, near the mountains. It was dark when we arrived. The air was fresh, and the mood was calm. I had been told of the beauty of the region, but because it was dark, I wasn't able to see it for myself. We went to bed, but when I got up the next morning and walked outside, my jaw dropped. The Rocky Mountains were on full display, spread out before us in full grandeur. The mountains were framed with clouds that brought new revelation to the color silver. I was stopped in my tracks by the glorious reality of the beautiful surrounding. It was breathtaking.

Though it had gone unseen the night before, that didn't mean it was not present. But when what was present was revealed to me, it changed my perspective. As the apostle Paul writes in Ephesians 1:8–9, "With all wisdom and understanding, [God] made known [revealed] to us the mystery of his will according to his good pleasure, which he purposed in Christ."

Vision Realized in Prayer

Business plans and mission statements have reduced the idea of vision to a simple list of corporate commitments. But as we saw with Dave and Kate, the vision we're recommending in marriage is a *joint vision* that is only revealed in prayer. A marriage vision isn't one that is handcrafted in a brainstorm meeting. Marriage vision is a calling delivered by the Lord.

Vision as revealed throughout the Scriptures wasn't a small group of disciples sitting down in a boardroom and brainstorming ideas. No, it started with a people desperately seeking God, pursuing with persistence until the Lord delivered.

Acts 1 and 2 tell us how, after Jesus' crucifixion and resurrection, the disciples followed His instructions before His ascension and waited on the gift the Father had promised. They returned to their upper room in Jerusalem, and for ten days they "joined together constantly in prayer" (Acts 1:14). The disciples had a ten-day detox from their personal wants and individual plans. For days, they persisted in prayer and fasting, asking the Lord for instructions and clarity for their next steps. On that tenth day— the day of Pentecost—they saw a vision of "tongues of fire" on their heads, and they were all "filled with the Holy Spirit" (Acts 2:3–4).

The disciples of Jesus first did the work of letting go of their plans, and then they were filled with a new vision. That's when Peter stood up and spoke for the disciples to the crowd of onlookers. He quoted the prophet of old from Joel 2: "'In the last days, God says, I will pour out my Spirit on all people. Your sons and daughters will prophesy, your young men will see visions, your old men will dream dreams. Even on my servants, both men and women, I will pour out my Spirit in those days, and they will prophesy'" (Acts 2:17–18).

The disciples had done great things in the previous days. But something powerful happens when you let go of your vision for you and grab hold of God's vision for you. You go from your wants to God's dream. Might I have the audacity to speak the words of my namesake, the prophet Joel, over you as you read this book today? Perhaps God has something to say, which you haven't grasped yet because the grip of self-focus still has a hold on your soul. Don't be so captivated by a vision for self that you can't step into a vision for your marriage.

The American Dream is about pursuing what you want.

The biblical vision is about pursuing a God-given dream. It wasn't Peter who came up with the idea to share the gospel with the Gentiles in Acts 10. He was given a God-inspired vision.

PRAYER PROMPT: Ask the Lord to begin to free you from your personal desires and individual plans so He can reveal a shared vision with your spouse.

Nina and I really wrestled with vision for our marriage. It wasn't a date-night conversation—and done. It was many conversations and questions—and even the conflicts we endured that forced us to communicate about our individual priorities and how to bring them together. Ultimately, it was grappling with God over His purpose for who we are as a couple and how He wanted to use us together. In other words, our vision was conceived and realized in prayer.

Prayer forces us to expand our understanding, to envision something bigger than ourselves. Through prayer, the Holy Spirit brings conviction, understanding, and evaluation and speaks to us in areas we've held back from Him and others for so long.

According to Nehemiah, a young man we had counseled in preparation for his marriage to Jaymi, the power of prayer can change perspective. He told us, "Prayer has helped me realize I have two visions in life: a selfish vision and a godly vision. The first is one of comfort and control and security. But the second is concerned with principle and purpose and others. It's when I stop praying that I lose sight of His vision and start trying to control things, worry about things, and think about the tempo-rary. But when I'm on my knees, my true vision comes back into clarity. Prayer has become my anchor point that draws me back to healthy vision."

If you say, "I don't have a vision for our marriage," I'd ask you, "How many hours have you invested in prayer?" Let this be your place to start.

Vision through Persistence in Prayer

In the Scriptures, each time vision was granted, it was given from God. Often when God starts stirring, you don't know what He has in the works. But when you let go of your plans and begin to seek God together in prayer, God will form and reveal His purposes.

A passage in Mark's gospel tells of a miracle Jesus performed. In Mark 8, Jesus pulls a blind man out of his routine and takes him outside the city. He puts mud on his eyes and touches him. The man experiences a miracle and gains his sight! But when Jesus asked him what he saw, the blind man responded in verse 24, "I see people; they look like trees walking around." He could see, but his sight was blurry.

This can be a theologically troubling passage for those who believe in the omnipotence and omniscience of Jesus. Why would Jesus ask the blind man what he saw if He is all-powerful and all-knowing? Jesus would often ask a question not so much to glean information as to impart revelation. Jesus forces the man to acknowledge the work of God on him but also to confront its lack of completion. He wanted him to come back for another touch. Jesus touched the man's eyes again, and he received clear vision.

I know that some of you feel like God has touched your marriage. You've seen good moments in your marriage. You have a love for the other person. But you also have frustration. There is confusion. *Is this marriage right? Why does it feel like we're pulling in opposite directions?* Your vision is cloudy, and if you're honest, it doesn't really make sense right now.

I suggest that God is not finished with the miracle yet. You have seen evidence that God is at work, even if it doesn't make sense right now. Maybe you and your spouse have felt a deep peace in certain moments of connection but can't put your finger on how to cultivate a marriage that will build on that strength. Or you've had stirring moments serving others but don't know how to practice mission on a regular basis. If you're in a cloudy place of confusion, we want to encourage you. Don't give up on your spouse or yourself in this season. Keep asking God to give you clear sight. In Mark 8, grace happened in the first touch when Jesus put His hand on the man to lead him out of the city. Sight happened in the second touch. But vision didn't come until the third touch! Don't walk away from your marriage before God gives the final touch.

Vision Revealed in Retreat

For any couple asking the Lord to reveal vision for their marriage, we recommend that they plan an intentional time of seeking Him and asking for a revelation of vision. Nina and I have found that a vital tone setter for our marriage is a vision and planning retreat we take at the end of each year. We get a sitter for our kids and leave town. We put our plans on the table, seek God, and process together.

The primary goal of a vision retreat is to seek vision from God. It's a time to get on our knees or to log prayer-walking miles. We always bring a journal to write down ideas and promptings. Inevitably, the Lord begins to stir something in us.

It is important for us to do it year after year. Why? Because we have vision drift, forgetting our goals in the midst of everyday demands, and it's so easy to lose focus. Also, if we're honest, each season calls for a different version of renewed vision. It takes tweaking, prayer, and consistent attention to figure out how to keep working together toward the same goal.

We strongly recommend an annual vision retreat for every couple, and here are a few things we encourage you to include.

Get Out of Town

Have you ever wondered how much of your day is just habit? Much of your day is mindless routine and repeated surroundings you no longer notice. Studies show that around 40 percent of people's daily activities are performed in the same situations. Initially your mind engages the prefrontal cortex in making decisions. But as you repeat the same behavior, the information is organized in your brain and shifts to the sensory motor loop, creating a neural signature. In other words, your actions become an automatic, unconscious behavior.

In a study analyzing how individuals form habits, University of Southern California psychology professor Wendy Wood explains, "When the habitual mind is engaged, our habits function largely outside of awareness. We can't easily articulate how we do our habits or why we do them."[9] We are going from the intentional response to habitual response. To get a new vision, we have to break a neural signature so we can engage in ideas outside of our habitual responses.

Go back to the scene in Mark 8 with Jesus and linger on verse 23: "He took the blind man by the hand and led him outside the village." Have you ever considered why Jesus led the blind man outside Bethsaida before He healed him? There are many theories about why Jesus would have wanted to lead the blind man outside the village, but He clearly had a purpose in changing his surroundings.

What mindless routine is holding you back from grasping a new vision? Is it your routine? Your habits? Your way of thinking? Is it where you reside? Mark Batterson often says, "Change of *place* + change of *pace* = change of *perspective*."

I tease him that I translate that phrase into my own food-loving tendencies. Getting a new cuisine is often what transports my mind. So I've changed his saying to "Change of *venue* + change of *menu* = change within *you!*"

No matter how you say it, the point is that you need to get out of your normal. Rent a hotel room. Borrow a friend's cabin or tent. Go to a new city. But find a place where your synapses can fire in a new way.

Jesus often retreated to places to pray. He did not allow the routine, the pressures, and the needs to overwhelm the connection to the Father. He consistently renewed His vision, separating himself from those demanding His attention.

Prepare Your Heart

If you want to gain a new vision, you must let go of your plans. When you go on a retreat, it has to start with letting go of what you want the other person to do and letting go of control.

Remember, a vision for your marriage will not be controlled into existence. It will be birthed into existence through the Holy Spirit in *both* of you. This requires preparing your heart before you enter your time together. Start your retreat by identifying those assumptions, experiences, or plans that you need to lay at the altar. Let go. Listen to God. Listen to your spouse. Be open.

My parents were an interesting case study in regard to grasping a God-given vision while submitting to each other. Whenever they were at major decision points in their marriage, they would separately go into a time of prayer. And they would come back together when they felt a sense of direction. If they didn't align in vision, they wouldn't fight to get their own way, but they'd go back into individual prayer. They would repeat the process until they aligned with the Spirit and with each other. There was no coercion. It was a process of releasing personal preference and gaining God's direction.

Take a Look Back

The best way to prepare our hearts is to start from a place of gratitude. Whenever we enter a prayer and planning retreat, we begin by taking time for a meal. We look back and remember the beautiful experiences, the sacred moments, and the revelations. It's important to set a tone by affirming who your spouse is, what they do, what you love about them, what you love doing together. It's not just a practice to make them feel good, but it's an exercise that helps you understand deep connection points as you take in the full picture of your unique marriage print together.

ACTION PROMPT: Plan a vision retreat. It may not feel like time well spent, but it will certainly be time well invested! Here are a few questions that can be prompts. You'll need to take some time to think and process these, so don't be offended if your partner can't provide an answer on the spot.

- What are those unique gifts, talents, and passions that God has placed within your spouse?
- Is there a moment when the purpose of your marriage became more important than having your own individual needs met?
- When have you seen God use your marriage?

Answer these questions together. Ask additional questions of your spouse to push for greater understanding. Do a deep dive into those areas of your relationship that have brought joy or a sense of purpose.

Grace prepares us in marriage. Sight gives faith to us in marriage. But vision launches us forward in marriage. Don't stop short of God's full and clear vision for your marriage. Don't be satisfied with the attachment version of marriage. Ask God to reveal your marriage print. Just because you don't have clarity yet doesn't mean God isn't doing a completing work. Your invitation is to press into His presence through prayer.

The blind man in Mark 8 would never be the same again. Why? Because he had received clear vision. We've got to seek

God for vision within our marriages! We often find ourselves subscribing to the self-centered, partially committed, compromised vision given by our culture, when God has something so infinitely greater for us.

Remember Apollo 13's insurmountable problems? They were stuck in space without the vision to be able to see their way home. They were disoriented, and that could have cost them their lives. Then they remembered a technique that had been tested during Apollo 8. They would use the earth's terminator, as well as the sun, to align correctly. The terminator is the line that delineates between night and day on earth. By gaining vision of a constant, the team was able to align correctly, to navigate problems, and to accomplish something that seemed impossible. Even though they were far from home, astronaut Jim Lovell viewed the moment when they regained direction as the turning point for accomplishing their mission. Vision had set their course. It can set yours too.

Chapter 2

War Circle

NINA

When I first went to work for the United States House of Representatives, the member of Congress I worked for was an amazing man of God who cared deeply for his family and modeled a resolute commitment to his wife. The congressman also loved our young staff and often took the opportunity to speak encouragement and wisdom to us. Sometimes when we had some time around the office, we got him talking and sharing stories or insight.

One afternoon, after celebrating a staff member's birthday with cake, we were all chatting. I was pretty new in my dating relationship with Joel, so I asked the congressman, "What is the key to a long marriage?" His answer was quick and direct: "It's simple. You absolutely must commit to fight fair." He went on to explain that conflict and disagreement will surely come in any marriage, but each spouse must make a predecision to always fight fair. "You can't aim to hurt or win," he said. "There is long-term damage when that happens. And some people just can't recover."

That insight has stuck with me through the smallest and largest of disagreements with Joel. We don't always get it right, but it's the bull's-eye to which we keep aiming. There are a few rules of engagement that can serve as predecisions to keep us fighting fair.

Conflict is one of the most draining and feared parts of relationships. Yet it is inevitable. We *will* face conflict with family members, colleagues or bosses, neighbors.

Marriage is the relationship with the most proximity, so it's very likely to encounter friction. Because we are imperfect people with a sin nature, we will certainly face disagreement with the one we share the most physical, spiritual, and heart space. Because our creative God created us as unique but flawed individuals, it will take work to protect our unity as a couple.

I am no stranger to conflict. In fact, it is part of my heritage. My maiden name, *Krig*, is the Swedish word for "war." As the family story goes, my great-great-grandfather (many generations ago) was given the name in the military and chose to hold on to it permanently.

In the early 1800s, it was often the case that when a man entered military service in Sweden, he took on a new surname. In order to avoid the confusion of having multiple soldiers with the exact name, the company commander would "christen" the soldiers with a new last name. The names given to these soldiers would often mimic words important in military life—words like *courageous* (*Modig*), *brave* (*Tapper*), *strong* (*Stark*), and *fearless* (*Frimodig*).

As time went on, it became more common for the soldiers to keep their soldier name when they were discharged from the military. My ancestor decided that our family would declare ourselves fit for war for generations to come. So it's no wonder that I have a readiness for battle! Joel and I have done our fair share of sparring.

Healthy Conflict

We would all prefer perfect relationships where we feel understood and share the same perspectives and priorities. One of our favorite definitions of marriage is "an unconditional commitment to an imperfect person."

Conflict is not bad, but it needs to be *healthy*.

Rather than striving for a perfect relationship, we can strive for a healthy relationship. One that refines us, makes us our best selves. We can ask the Lord to use the trials in our marriage to grow us.

God's Word promises us that God will bring His work in our lives to completion. My favorite verse in the Bible proclaims this promise: "I am sure of this, that he who began a good work in you will bring it to completion at the day of Jesus Christ" (Philippians 1:6 ESV). God will often use our relationships with others, including our spouse, as a part of this process.

We challenge you to rethink the purpose of conflict in your marriage. Rather than thinking of it as an obstacle, what if you regarded the conflict in your relationship as an opportunity for learning? Conflict can't be avoided, but it can be leveraged for greater understanding. Over time, it can help you celebrate the ways your spouse is different from you and position you to do the work to bring greater unity in your marriage.

Persistence in Prayer

Understanding the important role that conflict can play in maturation doesn't make it any easier. Conflict can be painful. Disagreement can hurt.

Perhaps you are experiencing difficulty in your marriage that is draining and disheartening. You are pressing for the restoration of friendship and intimacy in your marriage but just can't seem to get there.

Perhaps the distance in your marriage is actually a very deep fissure that seems like it can't be closed. There are cracks that seem as though they can't be repaired. Tears that can't be mended. Habits that can't be overcome.

Be encouraged that these are the circumstances in which God does His best work! He is the Healer, the Overcomer, the Master of Repair. Problem areas are a testimony that God is waiting to write. Every problem is an opportunity for growth.

PRAYER PROMPT: Ask God to grant you persistence. Ask that He would reward your endurance with overcoming. Confess to Him that you need Him to do a healing work on the problem areas in your marriage.

Maturing Work

Commentators on our generation note that we live in a throw-it-out culture. Instead of fixing things, it's easier and cheaper to just replace it. This mind-set finds its way into our marriages, and we can easily drift away from a commitment to do the hard work of repair and restoration.

Our nature is to seek deliverance *from* trial. But deliverance comes from the maturity offered *through* trial. And maturity does not happen immediately; it happens through *perseverance*. And perseverance only develops when things aren't going right.

James 1:2–4 reminds us, "Consider it pure joy, my brothers and sisters, whenever you face trials of many kinds, because you know that the testing of your faith produces perseverance. Let perseverance finish its work so that you may be mature and complete, not lacking anything."

"So that you may be mature and complete," James tells us. Marriage is the tool that assists the process of our maturation. Conflict inside the safety of our marriage can actually be one of the greatest tools for refining in our lives.

We want the maturing; we just don't want the path to attain it. But we have to go through the trial. We want the reward without the work. But diamonds aren't made sitting on the beach; they're made under the pressure that's found deep underground in the mine. It's the exact thing that we avoid most that brings out God's beauty in us.

Know Your Source

To allow conflict to do the work it intends in our hearts and lives, we must understand its true source.

When our daughter, Ella, was in kindergarten, there was an outbreak of strep throat in her school. Each day, more and more children came down with the illness. Teachers got sick and classrooms emptied. As fervently as the school worked to clean and disinfect to restore health, the illness just kept spreading. Miraculously, Ella never came down with a fever or sore throat. I was convinced my superhuman mom protection skills were working.

Our youngest daughter was an infant at the time and had started waking me up at night, crying and pulling on her ears. I feared an ear infection, so I called a service in our city that sends a nurse to your home for an exam. As the nurse examined my baby, we chatted about the strep outbreak at the local school. When she realized our older daughter attended the school, she decided to run a throat culture as a precaution. Within minutes, the test revealed that Ella had a serious case of strep throat! She hadn't complained of a sore throat or a fever. She was happily dancing around the room. When I sheepishly called to tell our school principal, he declared, "Ella is the carrier! We knew there was one out there."

He was teasing, of course, but it was fascinating to consider that my daughter wasn't displaying any symptoms but possibly infecting her classmates with the illness each day she attended school untreated.

Similarly, the outbreaks of strife that burden our marriages often have a source we can't detect. It is hidden. What appears to be the problem on the surface is actually being caused by an unidentified source. It is through God's revelation that we can come to learn the source of conflict.

PRAYER PROMPT: Pray that the Lord would give you insight. Ask Him to show you the unidentified culprits that might be wreaking havoc on your marriage. Ask Him to help you see the true source of the things that are dividing you.

Any counselor who works with marriage issues will identify a few main conflict generators. Finances, kids, sexual intimacy, communication, and in-laws are often the most common. It is worth noting that four out of five of these conflict generators are circumstances that are shared with no one other than your spouse.

A recent study showed that 25 percent of adults claimed their most frequent argument had to do with money. Among the most common causes of divorce were lack of communication (15 percent) and abuse (13 percent).[1]

For the most part, the issues that trip up a couple hang around as lifelong but unwelcome companions. As part of marriage expert John Gottman's Love Lab studies, researchers found that almost two-thirds of relationship conflict is perpetual. Couples therapist Dr. Dan Wile says, "When choosing a long-term partner, you will inevitably be choosing a particular set of unsolvable problems."[2]

The greatest sources of stress in our marriage may not even be what they seem on the surface. It takes some digging to come to a full understanding of what is at work inside the disagreements in our marriages.

Family of Origin

A careful examination of our histories often offers clues to the true motives and perspectives at work in everyday interactions. Each of us is an extension of the story the Lord has been writing our whole lives. The events and key players in our history write a story line that becomes the narrative to our daily connections. We carry the expectations, beliefs, and values with us when we enter marriage—the soul print that is unique to each of us.

Perhaps an issue between you and your spouse is actually unfinished business in past relationships that echoes in your marriage today. Brokenness or hurt experienced in a previous relationship can create a script at work inside you that you don't even recognize.

Is it possible your response to a conflict in your marriage is actually a reaction to something you navigated in the relationships of your childhood? Every person has parts of their upbringing they admire and hope to replicate, as well as aspects they want to avoid. Different upbringings can lead to different approaches in how they communicate, how they resolve conflict, what they consider to be appropriate time and space boundaries, and how they show affection.

Unmet Expectations

If I had the opportunity to choose a superpower, I would choose mind reading. With the power to read minds, you might actually understand what your boss is looking for on that project or identify which food your toddler would actually eat for dinner tonight. Mind reading might help us get to the bottom of the reason our spouse is irritated at us.

Whether the issue is money, sex, family pressures, or anything else, the core problem of conflict ultimately traces back to unmet expectations.

Dr. Kerley Perminio Most, a relationship therapist who attends our church, has worked closely alongside us in our pastoral positions to help us support couples who are navigating conflict. We've looked to Dr. Most for insight as we counsel couples, and she reminds us repeatedly that when a couple experiences conflict, it's most often because there's a deep need that is not being met.

James writes, "Where do those fights and quarrels among you come from? They come from your selfish desires that are at war in your bodies, don't they? You want something but do not get it" (James 4:1–2 ISV). The source for our conflict is almost always not getting something we want. It is the unmet expectations that become the point of contention, causing fights and quarrels among us.

Sometimes a spouse may not want to admit their expectation because they feel vulnerable if they expose it. "It's embarrassing to admit the real reason I'm upset. I should get over it." Or perhaps the spouse doesn't want to voice the expectation because they think a partner who loves them should know what they want. "Why doesn't he already know what I wanted in this situation? We've been married long enough that I shouldn't have to keep saying it."

Many times, the source of disappointment goes undetected because even the individual doesn't realize their underlying expectation. Some things are birthed in us because of our histories or feelings we're not even aware of.

Unfortunately, our loved ones can't actually read our minds. But the Lord can reveal to us the true source of dissatisfaction. Our hearts can be known only through the intentional work of the Holy Spirit.

The more we are curious about the source of our relational conflicts, the more we can meet each other's needs. Ask God to reveal to you the deepest needs of your spouse. What if you tried to "get curious" rather than "get heated" in the next instance of conflict?

PRAYER PROMPT: Pray for the Lord to give revelation. Ask Him for a holy curiosity about the needs and motives at work in your spouse.

The next time you engage in conflict, take the time to let your brain relax so it can engage properly. Then ask yourself, *What unmet need is at work in this situation and how can I meet it?*

When you are the one with unmet desires, ask the Lord to be the fulfillment of those desires. Look to Him to change or meet your expectations. Psalm 73:25 reads, "Whom have I in heaven but you? And earth has nothing I desire besides you."

Ask the Lord to address your motives, to clean your heart and give you His perspective. Then, even though it may sound scary, learn to express your needs and expectations. Talk about the difficult topics you've been avoiding. Be intentional to inquire about your spouse's needs and preferences in various scenarios. Your understanding of your spouse's motives, needs, and expectations will deepen.

Discipline Your Thoughts

In the midst of a conflict, we can find ourselves engaging in a very unhealthy inner monologue. Our thoughts can start to tell us lies.

"He never helps me with the baby. I'm not even a priority anymore!"

"All she does is nag me. It's like she wants to change me into someone else!"

God's Word reminds us to guard our hearts, because it is the place from which everything else flows. Our minds can be like a train that, if we choose to ride it, will take our minds and hearts to a destination we don't want to end up at. In 2 Corinthians 10:5, Paul urges us to "take captive every thought to make it obedient to Christ."

Marriage therapist Dr. Norman Wright writes, "Your marriage is affected more by your inner conversation than your outer conversation. Practicing good mental hygiene when it comes to thinking about your mate will make all the difference in the pleasure you will derive from your marriage."[3]

The Word of God has much to say about our thoughts. Proverbs 23:7 (KJV) reads, "As [a man] thinketh in his heart, so is he." The apostle Peter writes, "Gird up the loins of your mind" (1 Peter 1:13 KJV); we need to put out of our minds any thoughts that may be detrimental to our marriage relationship.

In the moments when our inner monologue starts to paint a picture that isn't true, it's important to zoom out and do a reality check. Early in my marriage, I developed a prompt to ask myself a simple question when I found my frustration toward Joel creating a narrative that likely wasn't accurate. I ask myself the simple question, *What do I know to be true?*

I have shared this question with my girlfriends, and they echo it back to me if I start to convey a concern that isn't likely founded in truth. "Nina, what do you know to be true?"

My responses bring the picture into focus. "I know that our family is Joel's number one priority. I know that he would never do anything to intentionally hurt me. I know that he values me and our marriage." It is in those confidences that I would like my mind to find its resting place.

It takes practice and commitment to train my thoughts to ponder the positive things in my marriage and assume good intentions from my spouse. Philippians 4:8 urges this: "Finally, brothers and sisters, whatever is true, whatever is noble, whatever is right, whatever is pure, whatever is lovely, whatever is admirable—if anything is excellent or praiseworthy—think about such things."

PRAYER PROMPT: Ask the Lord for perspective. Pray that He would help you see things from a different angle, with a greater understanding. Ask Him to help you grow in your ability to direct your thoughts.

Routine Maintenance

My stepdad owns a 1999 Super Sport Camaro. He is very frugal by nature, and it is uncustomary that he would indulge in such an extravagant purchase. Dad has worked multiple jobs all his life and afforded himself very few indulgences. His earnings were always used to provide for his family, and anything extra allowed us to pursue sports or arts or attend camp or whatever else we were convinced we could not live without. But as we kids got older and began to leave home, my dad made a bold move and bought his dream car.

Oh, how he has loved that car! The first time Dad allowed Joel to get behind the wheel while they were taking it for a spin together was when Joel asked for my hand in marriage. Joel was smart about his timing. Dad would have more easily handed me over than that car!

Dad has owned the Camaro for many years at this point, but it is still one of his most treasured possessions. The Camaro has a protective home in my parents' garage. It lives snuggled under a cover to protect it from the elements. Dad routinely washes and waxes the car. It receives only the highest quality gas and oil.

What my dad knows about his sports car is that anything precious requires ongoing care. Cars require routine mainte-nance. Jewels need safekeeping and regular cleaning. Our bodies need an annual exam by a health professional. Important things deserve our best attention. By giving his car careful attention, Dad avoids car troubles and ensures that it will remain in pristine condition for a very long time.

Our relationship with our spouse requires ongoing care and

maintenance. Intentional care and investment will ensure that our marriage remains in its best condition over many years.

Positive Affirmation

Dr. Dick Foth and his wife, Ruth, have been dear friends and mentors to Joel and me in ministry, marriage, and parenting. Dr. Foth was a trusted friend of Joel's father when they were both pastors in Illinois. It was the opportunity to come and assist Dr. Foth in his work for the National Prayer Breakfast that first brought Joel to Washington, D.C.

Dick and Ruth have been married for fifty-five years. As different as night and day, they interact with each other with a deep affection and lots of gentle teasing. Dick reminded us how important affirmation is to marriage: "No marriage can survive without affirmation. I didn't marry Ruth to tell me what I am not. I know what I am not. I need her affirmation to remind me of who I am."

In recent years, there have been many advances in study of the brain that help us understand how important it is to affirm our spouse. Research by Dr. Terri L. Orbuch attests that regular affirmation is a key to a happy and healthy marriage. Her study followed 373 couples for more than twenty-two years and monitored their behavior. She found one important thing that happy couples had in common: they gave each other affirmation every day. She clarified that affective affirmation included "words, gestures, or acts that show your spouse that he or she is noticed, appreciated, respected, loved, or desired."[4]

This is challenging work because our brains are wired to hold on more to negative experiences than positive. In fact, our own survival depends on our ability to remember negative experiences. If touching something hot burned you once, you will remember not to do it again. Therefore, our brains have developed to register negative experiences immediately in emotional memory. However, positive experiences do not transfer from short-term to long-term storage as easily. Thus, most positive memories or experiences slip away from us easily. Scientists call this the "negativity bias" of the brain. Negative thoughts stick around, and affirming thoughts slip away. So we have our work cut out for us!

As you walk with your spouse over time, you are living with all the accumulation of negative things said or conveyed to him or her. The persistence of pain and negativity can accumulate as thoughts of regret, resentment, and pessimism. They are carrying the hurt not just from you but from their boss, extended family members, and former relationships.

It is only through consistent gestures of kindness and plentiful affirmation that a spouse can shred the persistent negativity that threatens their self-perception. What an incredible gift we offer to one another in marriage! We offer our spouse a defense against the pain and negativity that can cloud their fullest understanding of who they are in Christ. Take that role seriously.

PRAYER PROMPT: Pray for the gift of affirmation. Ask God to give you the words to cover your spouse in declarations that reveal his or her true self as God sees him or her. Ask the Lord to prompt you with the right words at the right time to encourage your spouse.

The Language of Love and Respect

On our honeymoon, Joel and I went to an all-inclusive resort in Mexico. Each night, the resort offered different activities to choose from. One evening after dinner, we wandered into a karaoke night. Always up for an adventure, we signed up to do a song together.

While officiating our ceremony a few days earlier, Mark had mentioned the song "Respect" that was Aretha Franklin's signature song. He was making a joke that we would need to remember that song when caring for one another. We thought it would be funny to choose that song for the karaoke competition. Now, while the chorus is fun and catchy, the rest of the song gets complex and very high-pitched. Not too long into it, we realized we were in trouble. So we tried to compensate for our failed high pitch with more volume—simple fix, right? But then the deejay slowly turned the volume down to end the song! "Let's thank the couple for their spirited attempt at 'Respect.'" We got the message that it was time for the torture to end. Neither of us have terrible voices but that was certainly not the shining moment in our music careers.

Little did we realize that this wouldn't be the only time we would stumble when it came to respect in our marriage! Counselors and marriage advocates have identified that in most cases, respect is most highly valued by men in marriages. Women tend to most value being loved, adored, and cherished.

I see this play out regularly when Joel and I ride together in the car. When Joel is driving, he likes to track the estimated time of arrival. It is his highest achievement if we can take back roads or use fancy driving maneuvers to knock time off the arrival time. If I praise him for taking a turn that saves time or making his way around a slow driver, he sits up proud and accomplished. When I criticize or begin commenting on his decisions, he withdraws.

This was supported by the research of Dr. Emerson Eggerichs, bestselling author of *Love and Respect*. In his study of more than four hundred males, 74 percent said that if they were forced to choose, they would prefer feeling alone and unloved than feeling disrespected and inadequate.[5] In contrast, women typically share that they would rather feel disrespected and inadequate than alone and unloved.

Even the apostle Paul seems to note this difference: "However, each one of you also must love his wife as he loves himself, and the wife must respect her husband" (Ephesians 5:33).

Create a Safe Place

Joel and I had been dating for some time when we realized we needed some outside support to determine whether we would pursue marriage. Because of our different family backgrounds and large differences in personality, it took time to feel confident about a decision to marry. Okay, it was also largely due to a good healthy dose of fear!

We both wanted to take the next steps in our relationship but realized we had some significant issues that needed to be resolved. Together, we decided to pursue pre-engagement counseling. It was unconventional because most couples pursue premarital counseling once they are already engaged and preparing for married life. We have since come to highly encourage pre-engagement counseling for couples who are starting to think seriously about committing to a life together. We recommend this healthy step because it encourages intentional conversation and examination at a critical time rather than wading into conflict areas while a wedding is already underway and family and friends are invested. Through this counseling process, we first discovered our different communication styles and the need to refine them so our marriage could start and grow well.

At the first session, our counselor pressed on some issues, and Joel began to voice some concerns. As he started to open up, all sorts of thoughts, worries, and grievances started to pour out of him. Once he got going, it was a like a floodgate of concerns.

I sat stunned and stared wide-eyed. I was totally taken aback. How could this all have been going on inside him without me having any idea? The counselor commended Joel for his openness and promised we would work through some of these issues.

On the drive home, Joel felt pounds lighter. He was smiling and giddy. "That was amazing, wasn't it? This guy is going to help us take an honest look at our backgrounds and the different ways we're wired. It's going to be *amazing!*"

My mouth was cotton, and I was fighting tears. I had just been forced to face months of grievances unloaded in one fell swoop. It felt like a big load from a dump truck had been dumped right on my heart. Is this really the way he felt about us? It felt as though I had been totally in the dark.

Over time, I was able to understand that my response laid the groundwork for whether Joel could be comfortable pushing further into hard issues. By reacting with defensiveness or tears,

I had unintentionally created an environment that made it undesirable for Joel to push into areas that could cause friction.

The work we did in those sessions has set the stage for our entire marriage. Our counselor helped us understand how we each have a responsibility to create a safe place for the other to be open and honest about our true concerns. We learned to posture ourselves to receive so that we could have transparency in our relationship. I owned my responsibility to enter in to that intentional place of transparency and trust.

Joel continues to be very private and can tend to have many things working themselves out inside of him. I've developed an internal monologue that reminds me to withhold response right away and then to respond carefully, choosing my words and reactions. I don't always get it right. I'm so grateful that we've established a deep trust with each other and can share transparently.

To be our spouse's safe place, we must make ourselves approachable. We must listen to our spouse without judging, criticizing, or problem solving.

Proactive Defense

It can be hard to come to terms with the parts of our relationship that are not as smooth. Often, when we encounter friction in our dating or marriage relationships, we deceive ourselves to think, *Surely it shouldn't be* this *hard*. Yet the truth is, relationships are work, and the relationships we're most deeply involved in require the most work of all.

One of the best things you can do for your marriage is to do the hard work to work through tough issues before they grow. This doesn't mean picking apart every little grievance, but neither does it mean tucking away every irritation or swallowing every quarrel.

The number one recommendation we give to couples we counsel in preparation for marriage is to have a regular touchpoint that is planned and on the calendar. Those moments can become the altar on which hard issues are placed and wrestled with. For years, Joel and I took a walk together every Sunday night. We knew it was a time when we could talk about anything on our hearts and hear from the other person in return. Knowing that the time was planned gave us the mental preparation to anticipate anything the other person might want to share. That weekly walk became a proactive defense against issues that could otherwise grow.

Here are a few questions we recommend that couples ask one another. Journaling the answers is a great way to see the way the Lord is growing your relationship over time.

- How can I be a better husband [wife] to you?
- Is there anything I did or said this week that I need to make right with you?
- Share with your spouse something you appreciated about them this week.
- Is there anything that happened this past week or that you may face in the week to come that I can pray about?

With a set touchpoint to lean into and work together on, conflict can be minimized. Disagreements will arise, but they will be diminished because there is a set time to do the hard work that will lead to understanding.

If you are in a season of difficulty in your marriage, one of the greatest steps you can take is to set a time each week to work together on the issues that may divide you. It may even be helpful to pursue counseling to allow an outside voice to bring clarity to the issues at hand.

It doesn't have to take a long time, and it may be wise to plan ahead of time the topics to address. A planned time to discuss ensures that hard work can be done apart from moments of tension or stress that can come in the heat of anger.

Do the hard work to ensure you are not dismissing or magnifying issues in your marriage.

PRAYER PROMPT: Pray for wisdom. Ask God for humility and insight to see things from your spouse's perspective and the courage to do the hard work to address it. James 3:17 reads, "The wisdom that comes from heaven is first of all pure; then peace-loving, considerate, submissive, full of mercy and good fruit, impartial and sincere."

Confronting Collision

No matter how intentional we are with the routine maintenance for our marriage, there will be the inevitable tire that blows. As hard as we work to keep conversation open and be collaborative partners in life, there will be times we just disagree. It is to the benefit of a couple for each spouse to practice healthy conflict! Disagreeing well isn't easy, and it takes practice to get it right.

While it may appear that some spouses have a greater willingness to engage in battle, in truth, even as a conflict escalates, all parties of a conflict are usually in defense or preservation mode. Individuals respond differently to what they may perceive as a threat. It is part of our biology to protect ourselves when feeling threatened or vulnerable.

It is the tendency of some people to become more confrontational, using an attack response as a defense. Others will respond to that same threat with an escape response, retreating for protection. Neither is wrong. Both are trying to be safe.

In most cases, withdrawal prevents or postpones a solution. One way to escape a conflict is to pretend it doesn't exist. Another is to avoid the hard work that would be required to address the conflict.

In our marriage, my desire to solve a problem pushes me to engage in conflict. Joel is a peacemaker, and his preference for harmony in all circumstances can sometimes lead him to take measures to avoid collision.

Perhaps as you examine these tendencies, you already see your disposition within the conflicts you face. If not managed well, either response can destroy a marriage—either from damaging confrontation or from avoidance that leads to pain and resentment.

Rules of Engagement

Throughout history, opposing nations that engage in war have established ground rules for fighting. For a long time, the rules applied only to a particular conflict and only to the parties involved.

It was at the 1864 Geneva Convention that the rules of war became an international matter. The laws that came out of Geneva and The Hague were to apply to all conflicts in order to "diminish the severity and disasters of war."[6]

Rules of engagement were put into place because leaders around the world came to realize that unlimited warfare was counterproductive to most objectives. Unfair fighting practices also hinder healthy outcomes in marriage.

Parameters for fighting fair are intended for protection. When the inevitable conflict arises in your marriage, a few rules of engagement can keep your conflict healthy and productive. We recommend that you establish some rules or boundaries for fighting. They can be revised or edited over time, but laying some ground rules can save us from the really hurtful tendencies we all have when we feel wronged. Ground rules can include a commitment to avoid using the words *never* and *always*. Maybe you need to commit to certain things that will not be brought up in any heated discussion, such as refraining from mentioning extended family members, refusing to use against them anything the other has confessed, and agreeing that neither party will use cursing, crude language, or name calling.

When emotions are inflamed and defenses are high, it can be tempting to raise all of the issues that have been building in frustration. Make a commitment to stick to the issue at hand. Conflict can quickly deteriorate and become unhealthy and unproductive when it gets lost in angry words and when issues from the past enter the conversation.

Let's look at a few other tools that will help when you stumble into the heat of a disagreement.

Develop Your Listening Skills

According to Gallup's StrengthsFinder assessment, I have "communication" strength. I care about finding ways to express complex thoughts and ideas. It means I often take time to develop well-crafted persuasions and gain satisfaction from convincing people.

Unfortunately, this also means I can get caught in the web of spending time crafting my own argument or perspective instead of listening to the perspectives of others. I need lots of practice refining my listening skills, in keeping with this biblical reminder: "Everyone should be quick to listen, slow to speak and slow to become angry" (James 1:19).

One of the greatest desires in marriage is the desire to feel understood. And that takes listening and reflection. In an argument, instead of listening to the other person and truly seeking to understand, it can be easy to start building a five-part presentation in our heads. Instead of asking clarifying questions, we are prepping the zinger we plan to send their way.

A great zinger will never bring reconciliation to an argument. Instead of preparing that response, prepare the clarifying questions that will bring the greatest understanding. Try your best to hear the other person and then even repeat to them what you've come to understand. When someone feels understood, they become more inclined to understand you as well.

Soothe before Connect

What we know about the brain reveals the importance of *approach* in the midst of conflict. When we are stressed or angry or feel attacked, our cortisol levels increase and our ability to think objectively is hijacked by the amygdala—the part of the brain responsible for survival through automatic reflexes of the fight-or-flight response. The amygdala sends an urgent signal to the body to begin releasing hormones that will aid us in protection.

The amygdala is so efficient at warning us about threats that it gets us reacting before the parts of the brain responsible for thought and judgment can measure our response for appropriateness. In other words, our brains are wired in such a way as to move us to action before we properly consider the consequences.

In a conflict, we may tend to try to use logic to address a person in stress. But our spouse's brain has passed over the executive function of the brain, and logic is not easily accessible. Deep breaths or a break is necessary. Until calm is regained and emotional connection restored, resolution likely won't happen.

Of course, prayer is the ultimate reset. By taking a few minutes apart and using the time to seek the Lord, we can gain perspective. Remember, we are called to submit to one another out of reverence for Christ Jesus. In prayer, to revere Jesus is to reengage in humility. Ask the Lord, "How can I revere You in this argument, Jesus? How am I living out the call You gave us to love and serve?" Prayerful examination makes us resolute to reconcile.

PRAYER PROMPT: Pray for connection. Pray that you will use reason and self-control to be able to hear from one another. Ask the Lord to lead you in ways that help you override physical responses that come in flares of anger.

Interrupt the Pattern

I'm a problem solver by nature. I find nothing more frustrating than being stuck in a problem that doesn't have a clear or easy solution. The areas of disagreement with our spouses can be the most frustrating problems because typically the solution isn't an easy fix. Perhaps you feel like you've had the same argument with your spouse for years, just with different key players or circumstances.

In business communities, leaders understand that some of the most stubborn or persistent problems require creative or unconventional responses. Even children understand the power of play to help one think differently.

You likely won't have to go to that length to discern a fresh approach to conflicts in your marriage, but it's wise to ask the Holy Spirit for a fresh perspective and approach to find solutions to your marriage's most persistent problems.

In fact, God's Word shows us just how important it is to approach obstacles with our most creative solutions. We see throughout the Bible how the Lord accomplished His purposes by unconventional means:

- At the Lord's prompting, Gideon reduced his army to a mere three hundred men and yet defeated the Midianites by scaring them with the chaos of trumpets and broken jars (Judges 7).
- Naomi hatched a plan for her daughter-in-law Ruth to lie down at the feet of Boaz while he slept as a way to persuade him to take her as his wife (Ruth 4).
- David attacked the giant Goliath with five smooth stones and a little handheld slingshot rather than with armor and spears (1 Samuel 17).

- Queen Esther hosted a lavish banquet for her husband, the king, and his confidant, Haman, so she could reveal the plot Haman had hatched against God's people (Esther 7).

In each of these situations, God wants to show that He is able! He wants us to trust that His way is always better. Somehow we need to learn that our human understanding and responses are not adequate.

From these stories we are reminded that the Lord's ways are not our own. It seems that God prefers to accomplish His work with outside-the-box thinking. Let's ask God for creativity in reaching our spouse.

PRAYER PROMPT: Pray for God to provide you with creative response. Ask God for new ways of thinking and a new approach to long-standing conflicts.

Dr. Milton Erickson was a psychologist who understood the way a shift in approach could help his patients. Dr. Erickson was famous for his unconventional methods of helping patients gain a new mind-set. He would often use shock or surprise to interrupt the patient's pattern of thinking or behavior.

It is likely that, in your marriage, you have the same argument again and again. The same issues probably haunt your marriage, expressing themselves in different circumstances. Ask the Lord to reveal to you a new approach or response to the conflicts that lurk in your marriage.

For what it's worth, Joel often uses the shock therapy of humor to interrupt patterns of conflict between us. Frequently, as my frustration builds, Joel will use a well-timed joke or a play on words to make me burst into laughter, dissolving my irritations and reconnecting us.

Joel is very proud of this skill, by the way. He will often say, "My humor keeps us going." Of course, this produces an eye roll from me. But his lighthearted jokes have served as a great way to disarm my defenses and change the course of our conflict.

PRAYER PROMPT: Pray for new paths forward. Ask God to interrupt a pattern of conflict in your marriage.

Knock Down the Walls

We see this tool clearly utilized in the story of the fall of Jericho. The time had finally come for God's people to enter the promised land. The Lord had given Joshua word that He would deliver a victory over the city of Jericho but that it was going to require an unusual battle plan:

> Then the LORD said to Joshua, "See, I have delivered Jericho into your hands, along with its king and its fighting men. March around the city once with all the armed men. Do this for six days. Have seven priests carry trumpets of rams' horns in front of the ark. On the seventh day, march around the city seven times, with the priests blowing the trumpets. When you hear them sound a long blast on the trumpets,

have the whole army give a loud shout; then the wall of the city will collapse and the army will go up, everyone straight in."

Joshua 6:2–5

Joshua led just as he was told. The walls came tumbling down, and God's people claimed victory. The instructions to the Israelites were to lead with music, blowing their rams' horn trumpets on that final day of marching.

The marching orders probably seemed awfully counterintuitive. It would make more sense to try to knock the walls down. Or to scale the walls to the other side. We think it makes the most sense to go on direct attack, to scale the walls and use our best battle skills. Yet if we can get the walls to just fall down, we can enter the city with ease.

In our marriages, we end up fighting over all kinds of ancillary issues that seem like battles that *have* to be won. God's people thought for sure they had to conquer the city, but they really just had to conquer the walls.

Most of us spend our time trying to scale the walls. We never get to the actual conflict we desire to deal with, because we're too busy addressing the walls that have been building up for years. It can be family history or baggage from previous relationships, each of which adds a cinder block to the wall in your marriage. But when we lead with obedience, the walls are broken down so we fight the actual battle we need to fight.

I wish someone would have shared with me what R. A. Torrey wrote about prayer: "The reason why many fail in battle is because they wait until the hour of battle. The reason why others succeed is because they have gained their victory on their knees long before the battle came . . . Anticipate your battles; fight them on your knees before temptation comes and you will always have victory."[7]

Prayer is an altered form of approach. Music is an alternate form of approach. Singing, listening, declaring God's love and truth—these are all things you can practice to soothe your spouse and break down the walls instead of trying to fight your loved one. Next time you approach that place of conflict and the walls are up, adopt a different tactic. Shift from conflict to connection. You won't be able to properly reconcile the conflict if you can't first find meaningful, trusting, and soothing connection.

Circle Your Conflict

The best work of repair and restoration we can do in our marriage is through prayer. Commit to covering the hardest times of disagreement in your marriage in prayer. Don't wait for the darkest days to beg for God's provision and presence. Invite Him now into the everyday tensions.

In *The Circle Maker*, Mark Batterson noted that the crumbling walls of Jericho were the fulfillment of the dream of generations of Israelites: "After seven days of circling Jericho, God delivered on a four-hundred-year-old promise. He proved once again that His promises don't have expiration dates."[8]

He goes on to ask, "*What is your Jericho?* What promise are you praying around? What miracle are you marching around? What dream does your life revolve around? Drawing prayer circles starts with identifying your Jericho. You've got to define the promises God wants you to stake claim to, the miracles

God wants you to believe for, and the dreams God wants you to pursue."[9]

What are the areas of conflict in your marriage that you can begin to circle in prayer? Perhaps it's a persistent area of disagreement or a hurt you're having trouble moving past. Maybe it's a lingering habit by you or your spouse that is putting distance or distrust between the two of you. Or maybe it's differing goals that feel like they're pulling you in two different directions.

Now is the time to commit to a season of intentional prayer over the area of difficulty in your marriage. Confess to the Lord the areas of your relationship that need healing. Start a prayer journal and write the prayers of overcoming that you desire for your marriage. Write out a prayer of persistence and pray it out loud every day:

> *Father, I confess that I need You to do a healing work in this area of my marriage. Humble my heart, Lord, so I begin to understand where I can grow toward my spouse. Help me to release the past and all my unfair expectations. Give me divine ability to see Your ways of transformation and divine response-ability to act out Your ways of reconciliation. Amen.*

Chapter 3

Romance Circle

JOEL

*F*ourteen bachelors at one dinner table. That was my competition one fall night in the nation's capital.

I had moved to Washington, D.C., a year earlier to work with the National Prayer Breakfast. I was living in a three-level row house three blocks east of the United States Capitol. It was a house established for community with other young men pursuing God and their calling in the city. The guys living in the house hosted community dinners to which each resident invited coworkers or friends they had met. Its purpose was to provide an opportunity to make connections and develop a network of friendships.

Nina had just moved to D.C. to take on a new job working for the United States Congress. It was actually Nina's first day in her new job, and one of my housemates had invited her to come to our community dinner. Well, my housemate might have invited her . . . but guess who answered the door? That's right. The glory cloud fell in that moment. This other guy had been friends with Nina in college and had told us about her. He had shared how charismatic Nina was, but he hadn't told us how gorgeous she was! That night, she was seated across from me at dinner, and we immediately hit it off. We had an instant chemistry. There was clever banter, playful prodding, and plenty of laughter and energy in the air. Sometimes God shows up . . . and sometimes God shows off!

Love Is Intoxicating

It would be some time before we became a couple, but Nina and I had a spark from the beginning. Those first feelings of interest in another can be overwhelming and intoxicating. Science tells us there are chemical reactions happening in our body when we feel "chemistry" with someone.[1] When feeling an interest in another, an individual will experience elevated dopamine activity in the brain, which triggers the pleasure system and provides feelings of enjoyment and motivation. Another neurochemical, norepinephrine, kicks into action and causes the heart to race, the palms to sweat, and those flustered, blushing feelings to arise. Phenylethylamine (PEA) then releases physical and emotional energy and sometimes creates that dizzying feeling you may have experienced. For what it is worth, PEA is also found in chocolate. Yum! If Nina can feel the same way about me as she does about chocolate, I'm in good shape!

Together, these three chemicals combine to create a "chemistry" of love. It's an incredible feeling, isn't it? Your body synthesizing all the different factors of attraction, which then produces a euphoric and energized state in your mind and body.

There's only one problem. Chemical reactions wear off.

Chemical Force

Biological anthropologist Helen Fisher led a team of researchers that used MRI scans to study the brain activity of people experiencing romantic love.[2] The team captured the brain activity of the participant as he or she looked at pictures of the one they loved. They found that the dopamine reward system was activated and the participant became intensely focused on their loved one. In fact, in this stage, the brain patterns mirrored the brain patterns of obsessive-compulsive disorder. There was actually a chemical force driving them to be with one another.

One realization made by Dr. Fisher was that romantic love was not an emotion or a series of emotions; it was a drive. The feeling of love, the wanting and craving, comes from the motor of the mind. While she found activity in a lot of brain regions, one was the same region where you feel the rush of cocaine.[3]

The science explains the altered state of emotions we feel in dating or early marriage. It explains why breaking up from a romantic relationship can be so emotionally excruciating. It also explains the letdown that can happen a couple of years into a relationship. *Did I pick the wrong person? Did we fall out of love? Did that person change?*

But Fisher also defined the other brain systems at work in a relationship. In addition to the intense romantic love at the early stages of a relationship, there is also partner attachment.

Romantic love typically lasts around twelve to eighteen months and then wears off. At that time, brain chemistry is altered to maintain a more sustainable version. That's when partner attachment can become the sustaining force of the relationship. Partner attachment goes beyond the initial infatuation to the deeper, more abiding kind of love.

During this change from the initial drive to the attachment phase, some couples will separate because they've lost the feelings of intensity and drive. Other couples will survive in marriage, deciding to honor their commitment, but they just accept that their relationship is not what it could be. Finally, there are the couples who figure out that the relationship looks nothing like it used to be, but they can actually reap even greater benefits if they settle in to the new form of relationship.

In this partner-attachment level of relationship, a couple grapples with long-term commitment. Instead of obsession, the couple is thinking about companionship. Spouses learn to not just be driven by the desire to consume within a relationship but to connect and to complement.

For Nina and me, it was a shift from desperately wanting to be together to figuring out how to forge a life together. We had to make a shift from an easy, short-term blissful happiness to a pursuit of steady, long-term purpose and joy.

Extensive research done in recent years has shown that couples who have been in a loving relationship for an extended period showed an increased presence of the hormone oxytocin.[4] The couples who had been in a loving relationship for an extended period showed oxytocin released into their bodies. Oxytocin is known as the "cuddle drug" because it releases during sex, childbirth, and breastfeeding. It creates stronger bonds between people.

Studies have also shown increased neural activity in the dopamine-rich regions that are important in forming attachment and bond.[5] These findings reveal that a relationship can move from compulsive passion to deep bond. From short-term craving to long-term enjoyment. From chemistry to connection. From the rush of fascination to enduring romance.

In other words, we don't need to learn how to fall in love; we need to learn how to *grow* in love.

New versus Original

As our love has grown, we have not abandoned the romance that we experienced in the beginning. In fact, going back to that place of initial romance is critical.

As a culture, we are addicted with new. The fashion industry churns out new styles every season of every year. By the time we get home with our new cell phone, an announcement is made about the release of the next version. It's no wonder that this finds its way into our relationships.

However, God doesn't just call us to the new; God calls us to the original. We tend to translate *original* as meaning "new." But it's not. Original is the first place. It is that first place of vulnerability and trust. It is that first place of sacrificial love. It is that first moment of revelation of the image of God in your spouse. It is the revelation of the image of God in yourself because of your spouse. It's that first place of commitment and love shared.

In the Torah, we find the story of Isaac. The nation of Israel was experiencing a great famine, and Isaac was about to go down to Egypt to explore new opportunities when God told him, "Stay in this land for a while, and I will be with you and will bless you" (Genesis 26:3). Then God gave Isaac a promise: "I'll make your descendants as many as the stars in the sky and give them all these lands. All the nations of the Earth will get a blessing for themselves through your descendants" (Genesis 26:4 MSG).

Perhaps you recognize this story from earlier in Genesis. What God told Isaac is practically verbatim what God told Isaac's father, Abraham (Genesis 12:2). When I first studied this, I thought, *This is bogus, God. You ripped off Isaac!* I wondered, *Why doesn't God come up with something original?* But then it dawned on me. This promise actually *was* original! Isaac was being called to step into the original blessing of his father. He didn't need something new; God just gave him something fresh.

Isaac did go back to the original place—and what happened? "Isaac planted crops in that land and took in a huge harvest. God blessed him. The man got richer and richer by the day until he was very wealthy" (Genesis 26:12–13 MSG).

In the same year, he reaped a hundredfold. That's my kind of return!

The call to something new would have been for Isaac to go down to Egypt. But God didn't give him a new vision; He gave him something fresh and simple. He told him to go back to the original place of His word: "Isaac dug again the wells which were dug in the days of his father Abraham but had been clogged up by the Philistines after Abraham's death. And he renamed them, using the *original* names his father had given them" (Genesis 26:18 MSG, emphasis added).

After Isaac became wealthy from the well, the people around him began to quarrel. Isaac simply handed over the well. Then he dug another. Again people started to beg. So Isaac gave away his wealth again. He just kept digging wells, receiving blessings, and giving it away. My nature would be to hoard or to defend my blessing. But Isaac wasn't worried about new sustenance because he was connected with the original source.

We are so fixated on the new, but God calls us to the original! We have forgotten that place of original blessing.

A key to connection in your marriage is to revisit the original things God did in you as a couple. What's your origin story? What are the plotlines and memorable details that gave your story its very first sparks? Over time, we have a tendency to copycat other couples. We begin to mimic the lives and expectations and habits of other marriages. But nobody cares to see a second print of the *Mona Lisa*. People will travel to Paris to get a glimpse of the original.

Not only has God handcrafted you as an individual, but when you come together in union before Him, God stamps a unique original story on you as a couple. That place of origin is both a powerful force to others, as well as internally in your own relationship.

What is the original place of blessing in your relationship? Perhaps it's a significant location, an idea, or a calling. If Nina and I ever go back to Lauriol Plaza in downtown D.C., we have an instant spark. Lauriol Plaza was the Mexican restaurant where we had our first official date. It was a night of blushing and sweaty palms and awkward attempts at humor. I took Nina back there for dinner again the night I proposed. Another night of sweaty palms, excitement, and nerves.

Nina and I travel often to other countries for missions work. Each trip is a celebration of a time of original blessing. Early in our dating relationship, I led a team to Barbados to work with Teen Challenge, a Christ-centered rehabilitation center for people trying to come out of life-controlling addictions. Nina came along as a member of the team. Doing farmwork in 100-degree heat all day and then emotionally and spiritually engaging hurting people all evening have a way of bonding a new couple. We had an expedited chance to see each other tested and stretched. We saw each other's commitment to serve. The pressure cooker of that trip showed us how much we valued working together on behalf of other people. That trip became a place of original blessing for us. We love to travel for mission work together. Each trip we take now is an altar of remembrance.

Prayer Prompt of Remembrance: Ask the Lord to show you the original places and moments of your relationship. Write them down for remembrance. Consider a way you'll revisit the original places or moments in your relationship.

Renewing Covenant

In faith, the Scriptures mandate one specific practice to return to a place of original blessing. It's called the Lord's Table, Communion, or the Eucharist. It's a practice of eating the bread and drinking from the cup, which represents the body of Christ broken for us and the blood of Christ shed for us. Our faith is built on the foundation of the death and resurrection of Jesus. Every time we commune by consuming the elements, we are remembering and celebrating the blessing that God has given to us. It is one of the most sacred renewals of covenant with God.

In Genesis 2:24, we read that the marriage covenant is initiated as husband and wife come together as one: "That is why a man leaves his father and mother and is united to his wife, and they become one flesh." The most sacred act to renew the covenant, the original place of blessing within your relationship, is to have sex with your spouse. It is a powerful, God-created way to help give your entire self to another human being. It is a one-flesh connection.

Because the church has held up sex as a sacred act, there have been times when sex has become a conversation to be avoided instead of an act to be celebrated. Our culture has done quite a job of twisting the meaning and purpose of sex. We've distorted sex and made it an act of pleasing ourselves with or through another. But there is no greater act of communion and celebration, no greater reminder of covenant and blessing, than to bring our bodies, minds, and spirits together as one. Our culture views sex as an act of self-enjoyment with a willing participant. But its true intention is giving and receiving within a deep and covenanted relationship.

When we approach the Eucharist, we do so with sincere intentionality. We are careful to fully appreciate and give ourselves to the process of celebration in gratitude to Christ. Sex is designed to elicit the same purposeful practice. Intimacy through sex is intended to bring joy to your body and soul. It offers a physical, emotional, and spiritual experience. Song of Songs is an entire book of the Bible that points toward love for and enjoyment of your spouse.

I thank God every time I renew our covenant of marriage! It is the most intimate display of commitment to my spouse.

How often do you get naked? And I'm not just asking how often you perform the act of sex. How often do you share your innermost naked emotions? When is the last time you revealed the depths of your spiritual soul to your partner? When did you last share your pains, convictions, and desires? Your goal in marriage is to know and to be known intimately by another.

To get practical, how do you spell intimacy? Some spell it S-E-X; others spell it T-A-L-K. How are you intentionally getting to know your spouse and connecting with him or her on an emotional, physical, and spiritual level? By failing to be attuned to the needs of your spouse, you can actually push them away instead of pulling them closer. Sex can bring pleasure, or it can bring pain. You are engaging with your loved one's insecurities, their past, their most guarded places. Physical intimacy in marriage offers the opportunity to heal and to connect when approached with sensitivity to one another's needs.

Author Sheila Wray Gregoire talks about our differences as men and women as a healthy cycle for love and affection. "Men make love to feel loved, while women need to feel loved to make love. It seems like a recipe for disaster! But perhaps it makes sense. For each to get our deepest need met, we have to reach out to the other."[6] She explains it in more detail speaking to women: "When you are tired and you say yes, he feels close to us. That makes him release oxytocin (the bonding hormone), which makes him feel lovey-dovey towards us. That helps us sleep well, and then the next day he's often much more affectionate."[7]

Romancing your partner is more than bringing pleasure.

It's sharing intimacy; it's pursuing another in emotional, physical, and spiritual ways. It's learning about the other. It's caring for them. It's living out a covenantal commitment.

PRAYER PROMPT: Pray that God will give you insight, sensitivity, and creativity in the act of sex. Ask yourself whether you are pursuing your own wants or romancing your partner. Pray together, asking God to strengthen your intimacy.

We've established that intentionality is required to secure a marriage and give it the stamina for long-term endurance. How does a couple cultivate connection to secure an enduring marriage?

Make Time for Connection

It can be so easy to lose connection in marriage. Suddenly, you realize that you are coexisting, living in the same house but not truly connected. You cannot be truly known in marriage without doing the hard work to stay engaged in each other's stories.

As life gets busier, it's so easy for conversation to become transactional. For us, it was most noticeable when our kids started to grow up. "Who's picking the kids up from soccer tonight?" "Did you get the email about the class party on Friday?" Oftentimes, Nina and I will fall into a pattern in which all of our time together is filled with taking care of the kids, doing house chores, or catching up on work.

Every healthy and connected couple should make it a priority to stay connected. Be a moment maker. Consider ways to make time for activities that promote the most connection.

Intentional Conversation

To ensure a connected relationship, a couple must take time daily to tune in to each other's lives. Nina and I try to share about our day each evening while we're putting the finishing touches on dinner. We also try to go to bed at the same time whenever possible so we can share thoughts as we settle down for the night and drift off to sleep. A couple who leads a marriage small group at our church talks about the way they practice connection time as the first thing after arriving home from work. They sit in the living room for a short time to share about their day and their boys know not to interrupt. It's a checkpoint for their relationship and a sign of visual togetherness to their kids.

In theory, connection takes just a few minutes. However, in our home, when we try to connect with three kids, there are numerous distractions, sibling squabbles, and requests for snacks that make completion seem to take forever. But this small connection forces intimacy into our marriage. It conveys to our children that our relationship is a priority. It has inspired laughter, apologies, revelations, advice, and encouragement.

Most of us think of romance as wearing fancy clothes and eating a candlelit dinner at a nice restaurant. But romance is also humility and confession on the couch with the phone buzzing and the dog clawing at your leg. Can I get a witness?

The sense of touch is developed before we're even born. It is the first sense that our bodies establish. A baby has pressure sensors that let them know they are safe during a comforting embrace.

You have around five million sensory nerve receptors in your skin. When those sensors are stimulated, they send electrical pulses to your neurons, which pass the electrical pulse to the spinal cord and send it up to the brain, where the signals are translated. Physical touch actually incites both a physical and mental reaction. For instance, a hug from a loved one can lower one's blood pressure while also creating a feeling of value and importance. What's more is that you can't touch without being touched. A double benefit occurs in both the hugged and the hugger.

Jesus didn't just speak the truth of love to the people He encountered. He often brought healing through touch. At times, His touch brought a transfer of power; other times, a transfer of love; other times, a transfer of forgiveness. But His touch was a physical manifestation of an emotional or spiritual connection. There is power in touch.

Connected Eyes

Because of an increasing dependence on electronic devices, we no longer give each other adequate eye contact. Strong eye contact with our spouse makes a deep imprint.

Psychologist and professor Arthur Aron has spent much of his career studying love and romance. He conducted a thirty-four-minute experiment with varying sets of people. One version of the experiment had two people sit together and share intimate details about life for a half hour and then stare deeply into the other's eyes without talking for four minutes.[8] That sounds like torture to me. Or like a bad version of the no-smiling game.

Or maybe like an experiment that the majority of my guy friends would get annoyed at me for even suggesting!

The study showed that the connections were tangible. In fact, a few pairs of people went on to get married as a result of this experiment! We think that once we share intimate details from our past, we are done. But weekly intimate moments shared are constant reconnections with your spouse.

Healthy couples need ongoing moments of connection. The misconception is to believe that these moments happen only in a big gesture. While those big moments are important, it's the little things done consistently that create true and deep connection.

When I look intently at my wife's face, I'm reminded of her outer beauty. When I look intently into her eyes, I'm reminded of the beauty of her soul. To look into someone's eyes is to look beyond the exterior. It's more than a handshake. It's an outward sign of sincere interest in the other person.

ACTION PROMPT: The next time your spouse is telling you a story, turn your phone off, stop doing the dishes, or just pause to focus intently on their eyes. Have uninterrupted conversation while looking into each other's eyes. How did it feel?

Physical Intimacy

As we know, touch is potent stuff!

Yet according to clinical social worker and marriage therapist, Michele Weiner-Davis, research shows that one in every three couples is experiencing a sexual desire gap.[9] Frustration and resentment result. Though couples compromise and work together on finances, household chores, and family decisions, they seldom discuss sex. Typically, the person with less sexual desire holds the control over this area of the relationship.

Sex reminds us of our commitment and is a way to share intimacy and connection. Sex is not a right that gives us access at any time. At the same time, it's dangerous to withhold sex as punishment or use it as leverage to manipulate our partner. Sex is a mutual act of selfless love toward one another. When ego becomes a part of sex, the desire only to be pleased or only to please, some of the meaning is lost. Sex is more than a physically enjoyable act. A deep understanding and great vulnerability are associated with it.

Rather than asking, "Who should decide how much sex we have?" a better question is, "How can I learn to love my spouse in a way that meets their needs, as well as a way that allows me to share my needs?" Here are a few things to consider.

Learn How to Satisfy

One of the most sexual organs in the body is your brain. It takes time to develop an understanding of our partner. In general, men and women are wired very differently sexually. Often, men tend to be motivated more by sight and touch, and women more by emotional connection. Ask your spouse what romance looks like for them. Most likely it won't be your view.

Most of us approach sex just like we approach marriage. We primarily consider what will satisfy and fulfill ourselves. But just like marriage as a whole, sex with your spouse gets the best results when approached with a selfless attitude. If you only consider sex in the way that fulfills yourself, frustration will abound in both partners. But when you look to explore and adventure together, sex becomes a beautiful connection.

Intimacy All Day

"I wasn't in the mood. But once we got into it, I enjoyed it. Then afterward, we were much closer." This is the experience shared by many women. As author Sheila Wray Gregoire shares, for women, libido exists almost entirely in the mind. What women think about sex is going to affect their libido. Gregoire describes how our perceptions of sex can be twisted by its portrayal in entertainment. We watch movies, and the couple is panting. Their clothes come off, and they have sex. This leads us to think that the panting and arousal should come first, but that isn't how it usually works. Gregoire writes, "For most guys, they are aroused before they make love. But for most women, they do not get aroused until after they start."[10]

Nina reminds me often that sex is a mental game for women. She reminds me that it is the emotional messaging leading up to the day that has the greatest impact on our physical connection.

The tendency is to think that sex starts with a move, a kiss, or an advance in bed. In actuality, it needs to start from the beginning of the day. Throughout the day, there are little opportunities to serve the other. I used to only think of foreplay as touching or kissing just ahead of intimacy. But I've come to realize that the acts of service, the little moments of sensitivity, the little things I do to help or acknowledge my spouse, are building intimacy and connection all day long.

Consider expanding your view of intimacy. What if you slipped a note in your spouse's work bag? What if you used your lunch break to complete a few of the errands that have been stressing your spouse? Then surround sex with satisfaction. Give and receive a back rub at the beginning of your time together. Offer thoughtful words of affirmation and comfort afterward. Broaden your concept of sexual experience and pleasure.

Practice Planned Intimacy

Many couples are averse to the idea of planned intimacy. They're concerned that it will prevent sex from being mysterious and spontaneous. If your life is as busy as ours, planned intimacy is one way to assure priority. The things that are most important to us get first billing on our calendar. If you're not having sex as much as you'd like, set a time and protect it. Make a commitment that the chores, the deadlines, and the distractions will not interfere.

If you are in a season in which sex is not as satisfying as you had hoped, be encouraged. Studies show that the peak sexual years are between years sixteen and twenty of marriage.[11] In other words, sex can get better and better as you grow toward the other person. But it takes intentionality, patience, and innovation.

Be Aware of Obstacles to Sexual Intimacy

Things that hinder intimacy with our partner can take control in a way we don't anticipate. A large threat to intimacy in marriage is pornography.

Some individuals are caught in a habit of viewing pornography as a way of sexual satisfaction. Pornography can destroy the deeply intimate moments of your sex life. It trains one's mind to be aroused by an image rather than by intimacy with your spouse.

The struggle for the spouse of one who uses pornography for his or her self-satisfaction sexually is that it steals from the intimacy of married love. In essence, it's competition. Neither husband nor wife sign up for competition when it comes to their attention, affection, or love.

Pornography also impairs intimacy because sexually arousing substitutes create strong memories that the mind replays over and over again. The virtual replay of sexual images begs the question, "Am I the sole desire of my mate, or am I competing with other for a place in their thoughts?"

Pornography has addictive components that can drive a wedge between the intimate bond a husband and wife are meant to share with only each other. Satisfying yourself in this way halts the creativity and love that comes from a mutual sexual relationship. It is a regression from the vision of togetherness, reducing sex to a solo experience. A study of recovery from sexual addiction found that among the 68 percent of couples in which one person was addicted to internet porn, one or both had lost interest in sex.[12]

The full-on, unabashed sexual pleasure God designed a husband and wife to share is accentuated by a disciplined thought life in which our heart's desires are met openly with our mate. In our growing health consciousness these days, we are mindful of pure foods sources, pure water, pure air. Why not purity of thoughts devoted to our one and only heart's desire—the husband or wife God gave us to enjoy and to pleasure?

I've walked with a lot of people addicted to pornography—

people who love their spouse but find themselves trapped and isolated by their secret. Don't remain isolated in your patterns. Healing starts with honesty and continues with community. Take a step out in faith and remove pornography from your life to get back on track in restoring intimacy with your spouse.

PRAYER PROMPT: What is holding you back from experiencing deeper intimacy, connection, and pleasure with your partner? Ask God to give you clear insight to improve physical intimacy with your partner.

Seek Intentional Interaction

While many of us are committed to working on our fitness goals, education goals, or career goals, when it comes to building our marriage relationship, we tend to neglect the time it takes.

Make date nights a regular part of your rhythm. Predetermine a way to spend time together, just the two of you, on a regular basis. Anticipate that life's realities will try to stand in the way of your time together. Travel schedules, work deadlines, volunteer commitments, and family needs seem to conspire to thwart your plan. But you will never regret the time you spent to build your friendship with your partner.

An area of disagreement we've faced is the different expectations we carried into our time together. For example, we found ourselves getting into disagreements nearly every time we'd have a date night. Finally, we realized we were approaching it with different expectations. Once we got the kids situated, we would run to the car for our date as though we had just been freed from prison. We'd get in the car and look at each other expectantly. Neither of us had made a plan.

While I love the spontaneity of planning on the go, Nina would be disappointed we didn't have a plan. So much work had gone into setting up a date night, scheduling the time and protecting it on the calendar, securing a babysitter, and getting the house and kids ready for a sitter that she felt pressure for the time to feel valuable and well utilized. She wanted a plan about where we were going, what we'd eat, and how we'd maximize the time. She was convinced a plan would set us up for a deeper connection. I preferred to start the conversation of what we should do while driving away from the house. It felt like a grand adventure to go out together and see what options might present themselves. It was exhilarating to see where we might end up and what we might discover. Spending time to plan and set all the details for the night made it feel like work rather than a reward. It was a perfect recipe for conflict!

It has taken years of practice to approach time together in a way that is rewarding for both of us. We now predetermine who will take ownership of a particular date night, taking turns for planning and spontaneity.

It is critical to remember that there's a difference between spent time and sacred time. Biological research shows us that doing novel things together will increase the chemicals in the brain that affect romance and emotion.[13] Whether it's taking a cooking class together, going to a demolition derby, trying a new restaurant or making a new dish, or traveling to a new place, be adventurous as a way to create new levels of connection.

Sneak a Surprise

Surprise can be a powerful tool in marriage. Surprise also kickstarts the dopamine system in our brains, helping us focus our attention and inspiring us to look at our situation in new ways. Show up with flowers as you come home from work. Make your spouse's favorite dessert for no particular reason. Surprise him or her with a babysitter and a night out for dinner. Clean out the car when your spouse isn't looking. Make homemade nachos and set up the TV room for the big game that night.

I think I set a record for the number of anniversary gifts I've given that were returned to the store. For the first half of our marriage, I kept trying to make my understanding of what women liked fit Nina. For some reason, she didn't comply with my stereotype of women. I finally caught on to how much my wife loves to be surprised! It should have been a clue that she begged me to keep the gender of our children a surprise each time she was pregnant. When she was a child, Nina even asked her parents to plan a surprise birthday party for her! She still remembers how devastated she was when her brother gave the plan away.

It took me more than a decade to discover just how much she enjoys a well-thought-out plan executed to surprise her. For our twelfth anniversary, I decided I was going to nail it. I worked months ahead and took the day off without Nina knowing it. I found out her schedule and called those people to "keep their appointments" with her. I was waiting in front of our kids' school when she came out after dropping them off in the morning.

"Would you like to grab a meal with your husband?"

Her eyes lit up. "Really?"

After driving for a while, I turned and asked her if she wanted to have Chicago pizza for lunch. Confused, she asked where we were going to find Chicago pizza. Just as I got off on the highway exit for the airport, I said, "How about we eat it in Chicago?"

She squealed, "Wait, what? Joel, what are you talking about?"

I've never seen someone go through the five stages of panic to joy in two minutes flat!

"Hold on, Joel, how are we going to get there? How is this going to work? What about the kids?"

"I already have our plane tickets. We have forty-five minutes until departure. I have it all covered."

"Joel, no. No way, this is . . . the kids . . . have to be picked up from school. They have nowhere to go. Nooo, this is *not* going to work!"

"My sister is going to pick them up from school. Your sister is going to stay with them tonight. I put a frozen pizza in the freezer. It's all good."

"I can't. How will I have time to pack? We need to think this through. We can't . . . we need transportation there, a place to stay."

"I've got a hotel reservation and a ride from the airport, and I had your best friend pack a bag with extra clothing options—it's in the trunk."

"Well . . . [starts crying], this is the sweetest thing anyone has ever done for me!"

Listen, I've done a lot wrong. I've blown a lot of special moment opportunities. But I got at least one year right! We flew to Chicago for the most epic twenty-hour trip, and it remains one of the sweetest experiences of our marriage. Have you gotten to know your spouse well enough to know how to actually connect?

One of the formational books we read early in our marriage was Gary Chapman's *The Five Love Languages: The Secret to Love That Lasts*.[14] He explained that each person gives and receives love in unique ways. Individuals speak a unique dialect. One of the goals in marriage is to learn to speak the love language of your spouse. During his more than fifteen years of counseling couples, Chapman heard different versions of the same complaint over and over: spouses felt as though they were not loved by the other. Ultimately, Chapman recognized that what they were articulating was a frustrated desire. Love was not being communicated in the way they best received it.

Be a Student of Your Spouse

The effectiveness of your love is based not on your own experience but on what your spouse experiences. To effectively love your spouse, you must learn about your spouse. It takes focus and study to learn how your spouse hears and interprets, how they perceive their world, how they make decisions, and when they best receive information.

What if you got a PhD in your spouse? Of course, I don't just mean an education in their weaknesses. I'm suggesting a true understanding of their tendencies, their joys, their sorrows, their rhythms, their motivations.

Albert Einstein once said, "I have no special talents. I am only passionately curious."[15] Your spouse is an elective course you can attend every day. School is in session all the time! How many of us are busy skipping class?

Progressions of understanding happen when you're a student of your spouse. Early in marriage, I loved Nina in the way that came natural to me. Everything about her was new and interesting, and I wanted to know more. I studied to find ways to serve her. I learned that Nina's love language was words of affirmation and that it's important to speak life-giving words to her. It wasn't natural for me to use my words to show affection. But I worked to put this principle into practice on a regular basis to more aptly connect with her.

After a time, I realized there was a second-level course I needed to take on my wife—Love Language 201. I couldn't help but notice that the words I spoke seemed to fall a little flat. I'd tell her I loved her every chance I'd get and that she was beautiful. I tried to tell her in a playful way, in an adoring way, in a sincere way. She would thank me, but it didn't seem to make much difference. I wondered, *Where am I going wrong? I thought words of affirmation are her love language? I am trying here!*

Clarity came when Nina shared with me her results after taking Gallup's StrengthsFinder survey.[16] Based on a forty-year study of human strengths, Gallup created a language of the thirty-four most common talents and developed the Clifton StrengthsFinder assessment to help people discover and describe their top five talents. On Nina's strengths list is "significance." As Nina read the description to me, I realized that she craved to be affirmed for things she had accomplished. In other words, I could feed her with adoring, doting words, but if they aren't attached to something that shows her significance, something she achieved, it has minimal value to her. Telling her I love her or affirming her looks were things that were outside of her control. But praising the things that Nina accomplished spoke to her value as a contributing person, something she values highly. Rather than saying, "Nina, you are such a good mom. Thanks for loving our kids," I can say, "When you challenged and helped Ella with her science fair project, you planted a seed of confidence in her. She was confident and well-spoken at her science fair, and that was because of the investment you made. I'm so thankful that you mother our children so well."

John Maxwell wrote, "The greatest enemy of learning is knowledge."[17] Whatever you know about your spouse, don't let it hold back deeper intimacy and revelation of who they are.

PRAYER PROMPT: Ask God to give you a greater understanding of your spouse. Do the hard work to peel back the layers of their personality and motivations to understand them fully.

We can rationalize giving in to frustration when our spouse is not connecting with our genuine efforts. Here are a couple of prompts to keep you learning in your marriage.

- *Ask questions:* Avoid making assumptions that you know everything about your spouse. Be inquisitive. When was the last time you asked your spouse a question that made them pause and have to think? Questions don't just offer you a window into your spouse's heart; they incite insight into your spouse as well. A good question forces a person to learn more about themselves. Jesus was better than anyone at this. He would ask a question that led a person to examine their motives and values.

- *Be attentive:* In an educational setting, seldom do you leave a class without taking notes. Studying the content on your own can be helpful, but if you don't learn what's important to the teacher, you won't pass the class. For my wife, purchasing an outfit does not impress her the way a well-timed cup of coffee does. (For the record, it's a skim vanilla latte, less sweet, extra hot.) It's not that a gift of clothing is a wrong gift for a woman; it's just that a gift of clothing is a wrong gift for my woman. She prefers to choose her own clothing and avoid the pressure to pretend she likes something if she doesn't. But there's nothing like the surprised smile when I hand her that coffee at just the right time. When you're aware and present in the moment, it's amazing what you can learn about your spouse.

ACTION PROMPT: Write down one observation about your spouse each week and then find a way to take action.

If you've ever had a moment when you or your spouse made an attempt at loving the other and it just fell flat, this concept will strike a chord. The challenge that lies within it is the work of figuring out both your spouse and your dialect. Gary Chapman suggests a three-step approach:[18]

1. How does your partner most often express love to you and others?
2. What does your partner complain about most?
3. What does your partner request most often?

Our first couple of years of marriage, Nina and I were missing each other in terms of connection. We loved each other but often didn't feel loved by the other. Nina is a person who appreciates words, both speaking them and hearing them. I think she often has three times my word count per day because she speaks faster, gives more of the story, and just has better things to say than I do!

I could go a long time without hearing Nina tell me "I love you," and I might not notice. Nina asked me what my love language is, and I told her "food." I received one of those loving eye rolls that comes my way when I joke at a time when I'm supposed to be connecting. She told me that food was *not* a love language. I said, "I guess it depends what kind of dialect you speak—I happen to speak New York strip!" From what I recall, she didn't laugh.

But if I had to live in the constructs of Dr. Chapman's categories, I'd say that acts of service is the sweet spot for me. If Nina helps me with a project or makes a smoothie in the morning for me, those simple ways to serve make me feel like she genuinely loves me. When you find that place where your spouse truly finds joy and love, it's like a valve opening up and all the backed-up energy for connection just comes pouring out.

Knee-ology

I hope that the biology and psychology of love in this chapter bring greater understanding of what is at work in our marriage. But I have a deep conviction that we also need to learn the importance of knee-ology. When our knees touch the ground in prayer, the Holy Spirit touches our hearts in power. There is no match for the connection that is forged in prayer. Beyond a passion for love or a pursuit for understanding, spouses need a commitment to pray over one another. One of the greatest forms of love is to call out your loved one's name to the Lord.

When we come before the Author and Creator to lift up our spouse, it is one of the highest forms of compliment and one of the greatest acts of selflessness. It is what will catch God's heart to move in your marriage. Commit to pray for your spouse every day. The battle for your spouse's heart is won in the prayer closet. When I begin my day in prayer, I am prepared to navigate our marriage with Nina's interests in mind. When I come to a place of friction or tension with Nina, I can draw on the peace that was gained in prayer that morning. Pride ends when prayer begins.

ACTION PROMPT: Consider visiting the original places of your love. What would it take to rekindle your romance, to ignite the passion and desire within your relationship? What steps could you take to focus on the needs of your spouse? Pray over the hidden places of the heart that are being held back from a partner. Ask God to awaken deep connection in your marriage.

Would you allow us the honor of praying over you right now? As a pastor, I believe that God can do something original in you and your spouse. Receive this prayer over you and your spouse as you grow in connection.

Great God, romance was Your idea. Nina and I ask that You ignite passion and desire within the relationship of the man or woman holding this book right now.

Grant each of them the grace to be sensitive to their spouse's fears, hurts, and insecurities. Grant them the courage to face up to failures, missteps, and addictions. Break them free from the chains that have held them back from deeper levels of intimacy. Give them boldness to take action to pursue accountability.

May each person focus not on his or her own wants but on the pleasure and treasure they can provoke and enjoy in their partner.

For those who are far from each other, give restoration. Give repentance. Give redemption. Do what only You can do to repair and reestablish their covenant partnership. Strengthen them to once again climb the mountain to meet their mate, that they may summit the gift of God called marriage.

Today, Nina and I circle this marriage. We circle sacred covenant. We circle the hidden places of the heart that are being held back from a partner. We call out Your purposes, Your goodness, and Your passion, which You have placed in each one of us but may have fallen asleep in us.

Awaken our minds to fully understand the gift that is our spouse.

Awaken our hearts to fully embrace the uniqueness that is in our spouse.

Awaken our passions to yearn for deep connection emotionally, physically, and spiritually with our spouse.

Awaken our worship for You, God, because when we reconnect with You, we are reminded of who we are in You. Only then we can accurately love our spouse.

Have Your will and Your way in our marriages, God. We ask these things in Your powerful name, Jesus.

Amen!

Chapter 4

Dance Circle

JOEL

*T*here's a tradition in the Jewish wedding ceremony in which the bride and groom circle one another. The bride first circles the groom three times. Then the groom circles the bride three times. The audience watches in suspense to see if one might sneak a glance at the other. In the finale, the couple clasps hands with one another and circle the *chuppah* canopy one more time, a seventh circle. The number of times is significant. Seven circles represent the seven days of creation, just as the wedding ceremony is the creation of a new household.

We introduced this tradition in chapter 1. It is called *hakafot* (plural)—a Hebrew word that means "circling." The circling is a prayer and a declaration in partnership. It represents give-and-take. This sacred moment is like a first dance of spiritual intention.

Similarly, marriage is like a dance. It involves merging interests, celebrating uniqueness, sharing joy. A couple forges new life together through distinctive but interactive movements. Each partner has to lean into one another and then lean away, depending on the other's stability. Then again, dances aren't always executed well. Partners can fall off balance and out of sync, dancing a different style or to a different beat.

Of course, we're using dance as a metaphor here, but dance is actually an important part of the beginning of our own love story. Though we had first met each other when Nina was invited to a dinner at the house where I was living, we actually got to know each other when a group of friends decided to go dancing one Friday evening. I didn't know that Nina would be coming along, but I was pleasantly surprised when she joined us. Little did I know that she was about to surprise me a little more.

Nina wasn't a dance novice like the rest of us. She somehow managed to conceal the fact that dance had been a part of her life for most of her younger years.

The group of us had such a fun time that night that we decided to sign up for a weekly class together. Nina and I later revealed to each other that we were both just looking for an excuse to spend more time together. The class was held across town, so we'd all meet up, pile into my car, and cruise across town in my 1985 Lincoln Town Car. Before you write me off, guys, that car was brilliant. Though it got probably five miles to the gallon, it also had bench seats, so there was no boundary between driver and passenger. Combined with the slick leather upholstery, all it took was one sharp right turn—and look who ended up cozy next to me? Nina didn't stand a chance! It's why I kept circling the D.C. roundabouts whenever we went out. "Oh shoot, missed the turn again!" Each week, that car would take us to learn how to dance, both on the dance floor as well as in a newfound relationship.

Counterbalance

One of the very first weeks of that class, our instructor instructed us about one of the foundations of partner dance—counterbalance. Dancers offer one another counterbalance by leaning in and out of positions that would otherwise throw them off balance. A partner shifts his or her weight or pulls the other, leaning away to allow the other dancer to create lines and pictures that would be impossible without the support of their partner.

Counterbalance uses the tension of opposing forces as each partner uses their strength to hold the other. It requires giving and receiving, listening and responding—a balancing of energies that somehow makes a balanced dance position.

Any movement during the dance requires the partner to adjust to maintain the counterbalance. It's a continual process of change and growth, adjustment and readjustment. It requires that both partners be aware and responsive to the other to ensure they can maintain the balance and don't come crashing down.

In our class, we learned quickly that this counterbalance was the key to making the dance flow. It wasn't easy, and it took a lot of practice. Similarly, counterbalance is critical within the dance of marriage. The cooperation of partners is what helps us flow and glide through life together.

Yield the Right of Way

In Ephesians 5:21, the apostle Paul admonishes husband and wife to "submit to one another out of reverence for Christ."

When we meet with engaged couples during the premarital process, we always have a session where we unpack this verse. Most couples read the passage and bristle. *Submission* has become a marital cussword. The word has been hijacked, misused, and mistreated. However, submission in the Scripture does not mean being forced to do something. It is quite the opposite. It is a voluntary yielding of one's way, a mutual submission, out of love for another and out of reverence for Christ.

The word *submit* means "to yield." When Mark officiated our wedding, he reminded us that throughout our marriage we'd experience many moments when we would have to yield the right of way. "You will be so glad you did," he encouraged us. If you were to drive down a street in D.C. and decided to ignore a yield sign, one of two things would occur: a major collision or a major confrontation! We're really good at long honking and loud expressions of emotion here in the nation's capital. Collision and confrontation are also what happen in marriage when we blow through the yield sign and don't mutually submit to one another.

We spend much of our lives concerned about who we are as individuals. We have extracted purpose from us. We try to dance alone. But those moves that can only be performed in tandem with your partner are so unique and wonderful. They don't detract from you as a person. They highlight and emphasize your individuality in a different way. But it requires you to yield to your partner.

One of our friends has climbed the ranks of the military and was recently placed in a high-level position in the White House. Even with the pressures of his job, Doug and his wife, Kate, lead one of our marriage and parenting small groups at the church. They share openly about the give-and-take required in marriage. In Doug's thirty-six years of service, they've been married for twenty-two years and moved thirteen times.

It is only through Kate's patient support that Doug has been able to serve in this way. Through the years, the demands of his job have required him to be at sea for stretches at a time.

Doug shares that he would never be able to serve in the way he does if not for Kate filling the gaps at home. When Doug was overseeing the federal response and recovery to three major hurricanes in three months, Kate was managing their boys' schooling and caring for their home. But Kate shares how Doug has taken time off from work so she can travel and pursue her love of sailing. Having once trained on an Olympic team, she continues to be passionate about sailing. She has been able to maintain that passion because of his commitment to her.

There are times when Kate yields the right of way to Doug. There are times when Doug yields the right of way to Kate. They have to counterbalance one another, shifting in each new season, redistributing the weight. Their mutual love and respect have served as an example to many young couples who have been able to see them do this beautiful dance as they support each other.

Marriage Math

"The two will become one flesh" (Mark 10:8).

When marriage is the way God intends it, the math doesn't

work the way we typically understand it. God's math is $1 + 1 = 1$. We think marriage is a 50/50 proposition, right? We each give 50 percent of ourselves, and together we make 100 percent. But what it really requires is 100/100. We each give 100 percent, and somehow it equals 100 percent. It means two people dying to self and becoming one.

What was your idea of marriage when you entered it? Did you imagine someone to share joys and trials with? Someone to make you feel loved and supported? The vision many have for marriage tends to be motivated by self-fulfillment: "I'm looking for someone to meet a physical or emotional need in me" or "I'm hoping to meet someone who helps bear the financial load of life." Our culture's way of viewing life emphasizes this perspective.

It's no wonder that so many marriages don't work. This perspective ensures there will be unmet expectations. But marriage was not designed to just meet your individual needs. Marriage truly requires a sacrifice of oneself on behalf of another. How do we begin to lay down our wants, our needs, and our individualism and pursue God's best for our spouse?

PRAYER PROMPT: Ask the Lord to give you discernment to pay attention to the shifting weight of your partner. Ask Him to give you wisdom about how to create balance in your marriage and to help you humble yourself and yield the right of way so you can best position your spouse.

Celebrate Differences

Royal Ballet prima ballerina Margot Fonteyn and Russian ballet dancer Rudolf Nureyev had one of the most magnetic ballet partnerships of all time. Fonteyn was a forty-two-year-old veteran ballerina, and Nureyev was a wild Russian defector who was nineteen years her junior in 1961 when the Royal Ballet invited Nureyev to dance *Giselle* with Fonteyn. The legendary performance was the catalyst to their powerful partnership. Much of their appeal was in the ways they were different. Nureyev's youthful, reckless presence and Fonteyn's technically refined elegance created a perfect balance.

In the same way, Hollywood's most famous dancing duo, Fred Astaire and Ginger Rogers, had famous differences. Dancing in ten films together between 1933 and 1949, they captivated with their dazzling, complex routines. The actress Katharine Hepburn once said of the couple, "He gives her class. She gives him sex [appeal]."[1] Astaire and Rogers complemented each other perfectly, and their chemistry could not be rivaled.

We often think of compatibility as similarity. But great partnerships are often made up of two individuals who are different in many ways. God made every person unique, and part of the joy of marriage is celebrating the exceptional traits of your partner. (I'm glad I don't dance like Nina, and I'm *especially* glad she doesn't dance like me!)

In the opening chapter, we shared that personality assessments reveal how different Nina and I are from one another. A day doesn't go by that we don't see our different perspectives play out in our marriage. One way to look at it is to think that those differences will short-circuit our impact as a couple. But our view is that our strengths are actually doubled. We don't just have five of the strengths from Gallup's StrengthsFinder between us—we have ten!

Some internet dating sites seem to suggest that if you have the correct formula for matching personalities, it will produce the perfect person for you. However, there is evidence to the contrary. A study at the University of California, Berkeley, examined the relationship between personality factors and marital satisfaction in long-term couples in their forties and sixties. The research found that over a twelve-year span, personality similarities were associated with decreased marital satisfaction. In some areas, personality differences were linked with greater marital success. Dr. Robert Levenson, who led the study, commented, "Different personalities may provide couples with complementary resources for dealing with life's challenges."[2]

This is certainly the case in our marriage. We problem-solve and perceive things differently, and therefore working together gives us a wide range of resources for understanding and decision making. This is also true for many of the couples we admire most. No couple exemplifies this quite like Mark and Lora Batterson.

Mark and my sister, Lora, are two very different people, and yet they have one of the most balanced partnerships I've seen. It took work to get to that place though. Both will confess that their first two years of marriage were really hard.

Mark and Lora spent the beginning of their relationship working through the tensions that existed because of their different ways of seeing the world. Mark is a dreamer who lives in the world of possibility, while Lora is levelheaded and practical. He is open and public; she is deliberative and private. While Lora is more cautious and measured, Mark is a risk taker, ready to jump. Throughout their marriage, while Mark imagined all the big things God could do in the church and the world, Lora protected all the things God was doing inside their home and their family. Nina and I have had a front-row seat to seeing how beautifully the dance of their marriage has played out. Mark is an incredible visionary, but because of his partnership with Lora, it's not just vision; it's vision realized.

While marriage with contrasting components offers a complementary picture, it doesn't mean that differences don't come with complications. Sometimes it can feel like Nina and I are speaking different languages. Here are a few tips that have helped us navigate our differences as we aim for counterbalance:

- *Remain open-minded about your partner's approach.* It's a natural reaction when someone is doing something differently to judge or resist. Commit to remaining open to a different way of achieving something.
- *When your partner does something that baffles you, express your feelings about the situation, not the person.* Choose language carefully so you're not being critical of the person. When you criticize someone's personality, the natural reaction is going to be defensive. Rather than saying, "You are so messy!" try something like, "I noticed the dishes are starting to pile up. Do you think we could touch base on a plan?"
- *Affirm differences while also communicating your needs.* Here's an example of what to say: "Something I love about you is the way you are fully present with whomever you

are with. However, it's stressful for me when I can't reach you. Can you try to keep your phone where you can hear it in case I call?"

- *Celebrate the interests of the other person.* Look for ways to honor and encourage the ways your spouse stretches you outside of your comfort zone. While it's tempting to just go your separate ways to pursue different interests, make an effort to step into each other's preferences.

I recently attended the funeral of a local legend and friend named Scott Dimock. He invested in thousands of young people over his lifetime through a high school organization called Young Life. He was also one of the founders of the Southeast White House, a ministry in a historically segregated part of Washington, D.C., committed to reconciliation, peace, and helping people cross the lines that divide us. Scott was married for forty-nine years to his wife, Marilyn. At the funeral, she gave us a glimpse into their partnership in marriage: "Scott loved sports. I did not. I loved music. Scott couldn't carry a tune. In our marriage, it was love for me to learn how to play volleyball. And love was Scott learning how to sing a little. These last six weeks, while Scott was in hospice, people would come over to visit and we would just sing. Every song we sang was like Scott telling me, 'I love you.'"

I can attest that Scott wasn't a great singer. But he learned to appreciate music because of the woman he loved. The sweetest picture of a connected couple is when each spouse comes to appreciate the things the other values and even bends to celebrate these distinctions.

PRAYER PROMPT: Ask God to give you a love for your spouse's unique passions and differences. Ask Him to help them shine in who God has made them to be.

A Perfect Partnership

Position One Another

One thing Nina taught me about dance is that stability and balance are core components to any dance. They enable the dancer to move through the motions fluidly. The dancer's base of support constantly changes as he or she executes different moves. As circumstances facing our marriage change, it will require a constant shifting to reestablish that balance.

In my marriage dance with Nina, shifting balance has been an ongoing process of negotiation through each season. When we dated and married, Nina was working for Congress. She loved legislative work, and it was a great fit for her—fast-paced, nuanced, working with passionate and gifted leaders.

Once we had been married for a few years, we were ready to start a family. After our daughter was born, Nina went back to work on the Hill, continuing to juggle the demands of her job with our full life. Eventually, the pressure of supporting our home and family, leading a legislative team, and doing our work together in ministry was too much. We talked and prayed through next steps. It was important to me that Nina not feel pressure one way or another. We concluded that she would transition away from her legislative work so she could give her focus to our family and to the church. Though she had been serving in a volunteer capacity, Nina made the official shift to work part-time leading our family ministry for the church so she could be more present for our family. In the coming years, we had two more children, and the church continued to grow and add locations.

Years later, when our youngest daughter started school, Nina started to wrestle with feelings of doubt. She had put her legislative career aside to support our family and ministry. With all three kids in school, she was feeling a little lost. Though she had grown our family programs across all of our church locations and built a department of staff people who shared a passion for faith in the home, she wrestled with whether she had stunted some of the opportunities she might have otherwise had.

"Deep inside, I wondered if I had given up too much of myself," she said. "Everyone else had gotten what they needed, but I wasn't sure I had. It was painful to say out loud, but I confessed some of my feelings of resentment to Joel. I asked him whether he'd be willing to make sacrifices to pursue opportunities on my behalf as well. Not only did Joel not hesitate, but he communicated a sense of calling toward my purposes. The relief and encouragement were overwhelming."

Speaking honestly, the fact that Nina felt a bit alone and uncertain rattled me a bit—not because I was insecure in our relationship, but because I know I have a responsibility as man of God to care for her, and I take that seriously! It was in that season that I had committed to a period of prayer over Nina and over my kids. I didn't tell her about my commitment because I wasn't trying to score points. I was asking God to give me revelation for my wife and to be able to speak into her with divine inspiration. I wanted to be a prophet over His destiny for her. Scripture calls me to love my wife, "just as Christ loved the church and gave himself up for her to make her holy, cleansing her by the washing with water through the word, and to present her to himself" (Ephesians 5:25–27).

I committed for a few weeks to pray in the Spirit over my wife and each of my kids every night. My hope was that God would give me the translation and the truth of those prayers to speak over my family during the day. At some point during those days of intentional prayer, I responded to Nina's question with conviction and shared my commitment to serving her and setting her up well. Amazingly, just hearing that I was open to shifting seemed to lift a burden from Nina. In the Lord's perfect timing, she started to get more and more opportunities to write and speak and to use her leadership gifts within her ministry role.

Positioning each other in our marriage isn't always perfect, and it certainly isn't always fair. But we remain committed to considering the other and creating room for each other to be best used by the Lord. We understand there are more seasons to come that will require more shifts. Our children will grow and need us less, and we will become more available to one another.

I am so grateful that Nina was willing to bend in a season in which our family needed her most. I know the Lord will bless her for it and continue to give her opportunities. I'm also so glad the Lord gave me the confidence to lean her way when that time came in our dance so she feels the weight of support and the strong sense of her God-given destiny. We've remained committed to giving each other a lot of room to shift and to always lend our weight to each other in different opportunities. It has allowed us to create this beautiful life where we can both feel included in the Lord's purposes.

Being for the Other

We must convey to our partner that we are for them—that we're on their team and in their corner. It's one thing to speak faith into your spouse, but it's quite a higher thing to stir up gifts within them. Championing one's partner occurs in very few marriages. Whether it's because of insecurity, selfishness, control, apathy, or a lack of effort, we don't often set up our loved one. Be a champion for your partner. Be a cheerleader, a prophet, and a truth-teller for your partner.

The apostle Paul wrote to Timothy, "I remind you to fan into flame the gift of God, which is in you through the laying on of my hands" (2 Timothy 1:6). You are uniquely positioned in your spouse's life to call out things no else can see. As Paul writes to the Romans, we serve "the God who gives life to the dead and calls into existence the things that do not exist" (Romans 4:17 ESV).

The word *encourage* means "to inspire courage." All of us have things that hold us back—things like fear, insecurity, and lack of faith. But we're an inspiration away from overcoming this undeveloped potential. What if you are that inspiration, that encouragement, to release your spouse's giftings? Pray up, stand up, and step out to see your spouse as God see them. Speak into existence those things in your spouse that do not currently exist but lie ready to be ignited through you.

Words of Life

We started this chapter with the scriptural call to submit or yield to one another: "Submit to one another out of reverence for Christ" (Ephesians 5:21). But preceding this well-known Scripture passage on marriage is Ephesians 5:18: "Be filled with the Spirit." Notice that it's a command, not a suggestion. You can't submit to one another unless you are first filled with God's Spirit. In fact, all of the challenges in Ephesians 5 and 6—worship, submission, leadership, parenting, spiritual warfare—are in the context of being filled with the Spirit. God doesn't call us without filling us and empowering us.

In order to be filled, you have to be willing to be emptied. You can't pour into a container that is already filled. Whatever you have in you must be poured out of you so God can fill you and so you can begin to pour into your spouse.

The Scripture continues: "speaking to one another with psalms, hymns, and songs from the Spirit" (Ephesians 5:19). Our tendency is to express kindness and love in the same old way. Originality is saying old things in new ways. Instead of settling for the routine, supplement your usual way of showing love with innovative expressions. Be active in this process versus being passive and falling back into the tried and true way of expressing your affections exclusively. Give fresh application to an old truth.

One of the greatest gifts you can give to your spouse is to call out their name in prayer to God. I'm convinced that half of the marital problems would be solved if each spouse committed to consistent prayer for the other.

When is the last time you spoke your spouse's name to God? God gives us psalms and lyrics to speak over our spouses. His Spirit will give revelations they didn't even know about themselves or about which they need a reminder. Your husband or wife needs your words of love, affirmation, and vision.

Wives, you cannot fathom the power of the words spoken to your husband. We need your honor, respect, and words of encouragement. Even if we don't give you much of a response, your words are powerful building blocks for our foundation.

Husbands, your wife needs your affirmation and affection. Be engaged with her, listen well, and mirror her energy and excitement or her worry. You will help her feel secure and not alone.

Through the Spirit you have the mind of Christ, and He will give you the words to speak to your spouse.

PRAYER PROMPT: Ask God to give you words of life to speak to your spouse and to put a new song in your heart. Ask Him to equip you to speak and act out the power of encouragement on a daily basis.

Serve One Another

We live in a city of thirty-five thousand registered lobbyists. People come to our city to build their résumé, and the dominant question in our city is, "What can you do for me?" or "How can you help me get to where I need to go?" But in the Gospels, Jesus presents a different approach. One of the most common questions He asked was, "What do you want me to do for you?" (Matthew 20:32; Mark 10:51; Luke 18:41). And He says things like, "The Son of Man did not come to be served, but to serve, and to give his life as a ransom for many" (Matthew 20:28).

Jesus taught a posture of humility and service. This is the posture we are to lead with in marriage. Many misconceptions about marriage are rooted in this area. So often, a person asks what added value a potential mate will offer them. Instead, the question should be whether you are willing to serve this person and make great sacrifices for them.

A mentor of ours, Pastor T. L. Rogers, always says to young couples, "You're ready for marriage when you've found someone you want to spend the rest of your life making happy."

I'm a huge fan of food. I can tell you the best meal I had at any place I've visited. Any special occasion for me is built around what we're going to eat. Thankfully, I have a pretty speedy metabolism.

As I was growing up, my dad had a philosophy about food. "What's mine is mine, and what's yours is also mine." The problem was that he was the fastest eater in Chicago. So within three minutes, he was done with his food and was nibbling off of everyone else's plate. When we would go out, I just wanted to be able to eat the burger I ordered. I wanted to eat every French fry in the little baggie I ordered. He'd ask a question to which there was no right answer: "How is it?" If I answered that it was good, he'd say, "Oh great! Let me try it." If I answered that it was bad, he'd say, "No way! You're kidding. Let me try that." I learned to eat in a defensive posture with my arms around each side of my plate. I was on guard so I could knock away any incoming forks.

Twenty years later, I met a beautiful woman named Nina. She has a different philosophy about food. "What's yours is mine, and what's mine is yours." She loved to share everything. Growing up in her family, meals were a sweet time of sharing. They'd offer samples to each other from their plate. "Try mine! Do you want some of this one?" Every meal was an expression of love. Her stepdad had chef training and was an incredible cook. One of the ways he showed love to his family was in the food he provided.

He offered everything from his plate, wanting his family and any guests to enjoy every bite.

When Nina and I started dating, if she made any move toward my plate, she quickly met my elbows and my grimace. She was shocked and a little bit hurt. It seemed so selfish to her. She expressed her disappointment but continued to offer her food to me, inviting me to try anything she had.

I'm pretty flexible and try to be generous in most areas of my life. But for twenty-seven years, I had been stubborn on this one point regarding food. It felt fair to withhold this one thing. Food was really important to me. No amount of correction, nagging, or emotion had affected me. Never had I been motivated to change my ways until kindness was modeled in this way. My wife modeled Romans 2:4: "God's kindness is intended to lead you to repentance." God doesn't force us, but He incites change through love and kindness.

The outcome I never could have anticipated is that when I give Nina access to my plate, she only eats a couple of bites. But then she hands me her plate—and most of the meal is still available. Little did I realize that by sharing, I'd actually get double the portion!

The sacrifice to which you will be called in marriage will certainly exceed the food on your plate. It will push you to the limits of your generosity and capacity for self-sacrifice. This picture of marriage is very different from the one presented to us by culture. Are you prepared for that kind of marriage?

In Acts 3, Peter and John were walking into the temple when a man lame from birth asked them for money. This was not an abnormal occurrence. Peter acknowledged the man and told him, "Silver or gold I do not have, but what I do have I give you. In the name of Jesus Christ of Nazareth, walk" (Acts 3:6).

At first, it appears that Peter and John have nothing to give away. But Peter gives the man far more than what he had asked for: "Taking him by the right hand, he helped him up, and instantly the man's feet and ankles became strong" (Acts 3:7).

Peter served the man in the greatest way. He acknowledged the man's need and met it. Is it possible you could be falling short in your marriage because you aren't serving in a way that meets your spouse's need? You speak words of life and encouragement to your spouse. You pray for your spouse. But if you stop short of becoming the embodiment of your prayer, you may miss out on God's miracle for your marriage. Peter spoke with his mouth but acted with his hands.

In chapter 2, we said that vision is critical because it gives you a sense of direction and drive toward who God has called you to be as a couple. Prayer and encouragement are vital. But at some point, God will put you in a position to be the practitioner of your prayer and vision. The composer Gian-Carlo Menotti is reported to have said, "Hell begins on that day when God grants us a clear vision of all that we might have achieved, of all the gifts we wasted, of all that we might have done that we did not do."[3]

These were all small acts of service to God that had huge implications for people. You think your small act is of no consequence. Yet your great successes are all built off of somebody else's small act. The power of a small act of service in marriage is immeasurable to the long-term trust that is built up. When we combine prayer and service, the natural becomes the supernatural. Remember, as in the story of Peter and this man's healing, that the supernatural always comes through the practical.

Last Lecture

On one of Jesus' final days, He sat down with His disciples and gave them a picture of true servanthood. During their last supper together, just before Jesus was arrested and taken to the cross, He stood up, put a towel around His waist, and grabbed a bowl. He adopted the attitude of a servant and began to wash the feet of the disciples—a job performed by the lowest of servants as a way of showing honor. Peter, understanding that it was culturally wrong for a rabbi to stoop to the level of a servant, tried to stop Him. But Jesus persisted.

After Jesus washed their feet and dried them with a towel, He said, "I have set you an example that you should do as I have done for you" (John 13:15). When He went to the cross, He taught us that to love is to lay down one's life for another. But at this last supper, He also taught us that to love is to lay down one's pride for another.

In this act of service, Jesus showed that love is synonymous with humility. Foundational to our most intimate relationship is sacrifice. And at the very end of the passage, Jesus calls us to action: "Now that you know these things, you will be blessed if you do them" (John 13:17).

I wonder if there is a blessing over your marriage that has not yet been received because you haven't gone from knowledge to service. From right to righteous. From hesitant to humble. If your love is not put into action, is it love at all?

In one of my favorite sermons preached by my dad, Robert Schmidgall, he says it this way:

> The day has come when we've got to stop asking, "What's in it for me?" and we've got to ask, "Where's the towel?"

We've got to stop asking, "How secure can you make me feel?" and we've got to ask, "Where's the basin? Where can I wash people's feet?" We are living in an age when people no longer want to be servants of one another; they want to be rulers. But remember this: you'll never learn to be a ruler if you don't learn to serve. If you're not willing to lay your life down, God is not willing to use you.

Flexible

Before it was trendy to choreograph wedding dance routines and put them on YouTube in the hope that they'll go viral, Nina and I choreographed our first dance as husband and wife. It was Nina's idea, and we kept it a secret from everyone who would attend our wedding. We worked on it for weeks. It was going to be the perfect balance of fun and funny.

We started with a slow dance so nobody would suspect anything, and then we slowly transitioned into some choreographed partner moves. The plan was for the music to abruptly stop—just as the audience was getting into it—and then an upbeat hip-hop song would begin so we could finish our routine with some pop-and-lock awesomeness.

Except that when the pause in the music came, the deejay hit the off button! He totally killed the moment, "Ladies and gentlemen, for the first time, let me introduce to you—Joel and Nina Schmidgall!" Ugh!

We were already a little frustrated with the deejay at that point. He had arrived late to the reception and was hurriedly setting up his equipment as some of our guests were arriving.

He was late because he had accidently gone to the wrong address. He had taken a cab there, and when he realized his mistake, he had to call for another cab and wait for it to arrive. This was in the days before Uber, so it was a long wait. I still don't know what kind of deejay takes a cab to a gig with all of his speakers and equipment loaded in the back. I guess when you pick a deejay based on the cheapest rates, that's what happens. Though we were awfully disappointed, there was nothing to do at that point except start the song and dance over.

We started from the top, and now everyone was ready and excited. Our guests still talk about that dance as being one of the most epic parts of the day. They didn't care that it didn't go as we intended. But we still facepalm the abrupt interruption of our master plan.

In marriage, the dance doesn't always go as expected. It requires improvisation and flexibility, and sometimes you just have to make the best of things. Shift your weight, lean into one another, and give your partner the support of counterbalance. Rather than being frustrated, leverage it into a beautiful moment of togetherness. It will be such a better memory that way. The moments when everything goes wrong will become your most fun memories of love and dance.

Chapter 5

Support Circle

NINA

*E*ach summer, we spend our nights and weekends at a community pool just outside the city where we live. We love the pool days filled with giggling kids, splashing sounds, bags stuffed with towels and dinner supplies, and suntan lotion rituals.

The moms chat as we sit in our lawn chairs, and our eyes dart around and count kids as they hold their breath and cannonball in the deep end. The dads stand next to the pool catching up and pretending to watch kids—but mostly talking baseball scores.

Our families have been friends for years, well before we all had kids, and most of us before we were even married. We taught all of our kids to swim as early as possible so we could enjoy the freedom of poolside chatting. One couple, who bravely had baby number four when the rest of us had tapped out of the baby game, still has to chase their toddler around the edge of the baby pool.

All of us are interrupted by requests for snacks or towels or to hunt for missing goggles.

We've all attended our church together since our early adult years. Long friendships are rare in Washington, D.C., due to the transient nature of our neighborhood. We all moved to D.C. from various parts of the world—Illinois, California, Oregon, Indiana, Maryland, and even South America. In the miraculous ways that God works his unexpected gifts, we ended up buying homes within blocks of one another. It is quite comical that we drive outside of the city to enjoy pool time on many nights and weekends because we all live in walking distance—within two blocks of one another. We swap kids for playdates and borrow last-minute dinner supplies. Texts fly in off and on throughout the afternoon: "We are going to let the kids run at the J. O. Wilson playground. Anyone wanna join?"

We know each other deeply. We are fiercely protective of each other's kids. We know the tensions in each of our marriages. We know the heartaches and worries each of us carries over this kid or that. We are highly invested in each other's families.

When I first married Joel, I had the misconception of a marriage as a relationship in which each spouse met each other's full needs. Now I understand that this expectation is an impossible load for one person to carry. The rich relationships that surround us are essential to our health as a couple. Supportive communities are essential for sustaining a healthy marriage. Friendships of transparency are an important part of a marriage support system.

When couples begin meeting with us to prepare for marriage, one of the first questions we'll typically ask is, "Who is supporting you in your relationship?"

Context for Community

We live in a strange time when you can live your entire adult life without community. You don't have to meet your neighbors or introduce yourself to anyone at church. Chances are you live hundreds of miles away from relatives and have moved away from childhood and college friends.

Despite being more digitally connected than ever, we are more disconnected from true intimacy than ever before. Even while being connected to hundreds of friends on social media, loneliness is now considered a health epidemic. Rates of loneliness have doubled since the 1980s. More than 40 percent of adults in America report feeling lonely.[1]

In his book *Flickering Pixels*, Shane Hipps presents the progression of culture from oral to print to visual to digital in order to show how technology defines our present age. "The Internet has a natural bias toward exhibitionism and thus the erosion of real intimacy," writes Hipps. "There is . . . a kind of illusion of intimacy with people we've never met in person," an "illusion of closeness with someone while remaining totally anonymous" with little risk or demand.[2] According to Hipps, this anonymous intimacy "provides just enough connection to keep us from pursuing real intimacy." He writes, "It's a bit like cotton candy: It goes down easy . . . but it doesn't provide much in the way of sustainable nutrition. Not only that, but our appetite is spoiled."[3]

In addition to the false sense of connection due to technology, we face geographical distance. The increased globalization of our world means greater connections with new communities, but it also means a larger disconnect with the communities closest to us.

Throughout most of history, community was embedded in the fabric of life. Generations of families lived in the same small town or village and depended on one another for economic, emotional, and physical survival. Now, a greater number of adults are living far from relatives and friendships from childhood or college. Researchers Naomi Gerstel and Natalia Sarkisian found that married couples have fewer ties to relatives than the unmarried: "They are less likely to visit, call, have intimate talks with, or help out their parents, brothers and sisters, or other relatives . . . Married people are less likely than single individuals to socialize with neighbors or friends."[4]

If couples aren't careful, marriage can magnify disconnection from others. A couple may find that they've created their own little island, inviting only the occasional friend into their world.

In her 2012 bestselling marriage research book *For Better*, Tara Parker-Pope writes, "Throughout history, family, friends, neighbors and coworkers have been important sources of social, personal, and financial support to married couples. But today, many people view their husband or wife as the primary person they turn to for support."[5]

Research also shows that having a large network of supportive peers may benefit the longevity of marriage relationships. In "Breaking Up is Hard to Do, Unless Everyone Else Is Doing It Too," Rose McDermott, James Fowler, and Nicholas Christakis cited studies showing that "the more supportive network members are, the greater are feelings of satisfaction, stability and commitment that partners have for their marital relationships."[6] Here is where the circle widens. A supportive community is well worth the investment and is greater in its influence than all social media combined.

Community Affirmation

Though marriage has drifted from the framework of community that was historically part of culture, the affirmation of community lingers in our rituals. Even today, our wedding rituals recognize the significant role that a supportive community plays in a marriage. The bridal party is a statement of the importance of community, symbolizing the circle of support that will come alongside a couple in marriage.

Joel and I had a ridiculously large bridal party. It was one of those situations where we needed to have everybody or nobody. So we dressed our clan of dearest friends and family members in bright red dresses and bow ties and positioned them all over the stage of the church in an effort to distract our guests from seeing just how many of them there were.

In deciding who to ask to stand with us, we used two factors. We wanted to ask those who had played the greatest part in developing the person we were offering to one another that day. Only my cousins put on talent shows with me each Christmas and knew me when I'd wear a Swatch watch and crimped my hair. We also wanted to be sure to include those we knew would be most likely to hold us accountable to the vows we were making that day. They were all such an important part of our day and an important part of our marriage support circle—and they still are today.

Many wedding ceremonies include a community affirmation, asking friends and family to verbally declare their commitment of support. After the bride and the groom have spoken their wedding vows, the officiant addresses the witnesses: "Every person present here represents an opportunity for love and support of this newly married couple. You each carry an obligation to be an advocate for their relationship. Will all of you witnessing these promises do all in your power to uphold these two persons in marriage?"

"We will!" the congregation responds.

Aside from the "I do" that professes the commitment of the bride and groom, could the affirmation of the community be the most significant moment of the wedding day?

Community in Scripture

An embedded community was certainly the norm when Jesus walked this earth. The family was the core unit of biblical society. Generations of families lived in close proximity and depended on one another for survival and stability. Extended family networks were both insisted on and essential for survival. It was every Jewish person's duty to maintain and strengthen those ties.

Jewish tradition honors the benefits of friendship as well. Friendship meant more than a social connection in the Jewish context. Friends offered each other protection, loyalty, support, and moral guidance.

A sense of peoplehood has long been a defining characteristic of Jewish culture. Jewish texts explain that participation in communal affairs was not optional but was a religious obligation. Membership in a Jewish community always demanded a sense of shared destiny, manifested in the obligation to care for other members of the community and in the joy of participating in the celebrations of others.

Even today, we see this portrayed in the tradition of Shabbat celebration. *Shabbat* is the Hebrew word for "sabbath." It is a day of rest. The communal aspect of Shabbat is highly emphasized, and it is always celebrated with friends and with family.

This commitment to community is the background against which all of Scripture was written. The Bible models relationship throughout. Most evident in His relationship with the twelve disciples, Jesus showed us a model of invested relationship.

In the book of Acts, we see the way the early Christians devoted themselves to fellowship, teaching, and prayer for one another (Acts 2:42). It was when the early church made a habit of meeting together, eating together, and worshiping together that "the Lord added to their number daily those who were being saved" (Acts 2:47).

In Paul's letters to the early church, he called believers again and again to love and to unity. In his letter to the Philippians, he spurs the church to respond to the love and comfort they received in Christ by extending that love and commitment to one another. Paul writes, "Is there any encouragement from belonging to Christ? Any comfort from his love? Any fellowship together in the Spirit? Are your hearts tender and compassionate? Then make me truly happy by agreeing wholeheartedly with each other, loving one another, and working together with one mind and purpose" (Philippians 2:1–2 NLT).

In our culture, we consider community as a marginal option of faith. But in the biblical culture, community was taught and lived as a critical imperative of faith. Each marriage was interwoven and interdependent on a larger community.

Circles Rather Than Rows

There is a phrase used in church ministry to communicate the important role that relationships play in effecting life change—more than sermons from the pulpit do: "Transformation happens in circles rather than rows." Coined by Pastor Andy Stanley, this phrase acknowledges that God created us for relationship. Attendees at a church service or a speaking event sit in rows. Information will be shared one way—from speaker to audience. When sitting in a circle around a dining room table or in a living room, all parties are equally sharing with one another. Though sermons are critically important to the growth of faith, words delivered from a pulpit give information. But it is from a circle community that a couple can receive transformation.

As a symbol, a circle speaks of unity, connectedness, and completeness. Proverbs 11:14 (NASB) teaches us, "Where there is no guidance the people fall, but in abundance of counselors there is victory." A healthy support community offers encouragement, inspiration, perspective, support, and accountability. A consistent marriage community can be a sounding board and a guardrail during the vulnerable times every marriage will confront.

Circles of Support

God's vision for change almost always includes other people. Marriage is no exception. Marriage counselors testify that a lack of support is one of the greatest threats to marriage today. Community accomplishes important safeguards for your marriage.

ACTION PROMPT: Take some time to consider who is in the circle of support of your marriage. Make a list of those you have invited to lift up you and your spouse. Do you need to expand the circle? What about the support you offer to marriages around you? Are you spurring other couples on in their commitment to one another?

The circles of support that surround us look different for each marriage and in different seasons. For some, their largest circle of support may be their extended family. Joel and I are unique in our transient city in that we have extended family who live nearby. Our children are growing up with the support of aunts and uncles and the richness of relationship with their cousins.

Others may live far from family but depend on a committed small group of friends who get together regularly through their church or neighborhood. Families in the military have learned to maximize the relationships where they're stationed. Hopefully you will form a circle of support that also includes trusted advisers, like a mentor couple, counselors or therapists, and your pastors. It is the circle of people committed to supporting your marriage.

Let's look at some ways to maximize the different circles of support.

Authentic Friendship

Friendship is one of the sweetest gifts, but establishing trusting relationships is certainly not easy. In her book *Friendships Don't Just Happen!*, life coach and former pastor Shasta Nelson shares about the difficulty that adults have in establishing and developing life-giving friendships.[7] In a study done in preparation for her book, Nelson found that 75 percent of responders said they want better friendships. They responded that they are disappointed with the friendships they have and don't feel as close to their friends as they want to. She goes on to share that doctors have gone on record as saying that loneliness is the number one public health issue of our time.[8]

If establishing friendship is hard in singleness, it is exponentially more difficult to find friendships when you are married—friendships where the husbands and wives are all compatible with one another. The friendships you bring into marriage often don't fit you the same way in this new phase of life.

PRAYER PROMPT: Ask God to provide the friendships that will best complement you and your spouse. Ask for divine connections with other couples who will strengthen and support you.

Finding a couple with whom you can have a strong connection is like hitting the lottery. Once a couple has children, the equation gets even more complicated. Does the other couple have kids who are similar in age to yours? Do the kids enjoy each other and get along? It is like practicing multivariable calculus to make the connections work. With these barriers, it's no wonder many couples don't do the hard work of creating a strong circle of supportive friendships.

In addition to the puzzle solving that is required to match your marriage with friendships that will complement you and your spouse, there can be other barriers to authentic friendship. We know that a commitment to vulnerability is required for any authentic friendship. However, the culture of comparison that is exacerbated by social media makes the barrier to authenticity higher than ever before. Pictures in our social media feeds give the false impression that other marriages have an ease that you lack in your own marriage, making it difficult to be open about the less-than-perfect areas in your own life.

The more private a person, the more difficult it is to be transparent. Marriage is an intimate covenant, and to let others have a glimpse of the less-than-ideal can be a hurdle. A very private friend of mine shares, "I don't want to be in marriage with eight hundred people!" Of course you're only in the marriage with one person, but we have much to benefit when we turn our marriage circle outward into our wider community.

ACTION PROMPT: Talk with your spouse about boundaries for sharing. Come to an agreement on how to be open and vulnerable with trusted friends in a way that makes your spouse feel safe and affirmed.

Committed Small Groups

Intentional community may look like getting involved in a small group at your church. Perhaps it means getting together on a regular basis with a group of men or women, or it may look like seeking out an older couple you and your spouse can look to for advice.

Michael and Julie know how instrumental a weekly small group through church has been for their marriage. Michael had grown up Catholic, just outside the city, an only child with parents of different race. Julie was the youngest child of a large family in a Mennonite farming community in Pennsylvania. Both of them settled in Washington, D.C., to work in politics, though they held opposite political affiliations.

The first couple of years of their marriage were very difficult as they merged their different backgrounds and perspectives. They faced a number of hurdles just trying to get on the same page with their faith. Michael shared, "Early in marriage, when we hit an issue, I would think it only applied to us. I would be too prideful to share with others. I wanted to keep it nice and contained, as though everything was just fine."

Michael considered faith to be something very private. Julie kept trying to persuade him to join a small group at their church, but he wasn't comfortable with the idea at first. "Once we started attending, there were things other couples would bring up that Julie and I had a hard time discussing openly with each other. There was such relief in discussing things with other couples of faith in a meaningful way. Those relationships helped normalize the things we were navigating at home."

Joel and I have been a part of many small groups throughout our marriage, sometimes as a couple and sometimes on our own. Each time Joel and I are intentional about participating in a group that meets consistently, we have found great benefit.

Interestingly, it's not just the couples or marriage groups that are the most meaningful support circles. Joel has shared with me about the encouragement he draws from talking with other guys who are trying to be honest with their struggles so they can be men of God and carry themselves with integrity.

He has expressed that some of the most powerful moments have come in the "sprint groups" he leads for men—small groups of guys that meet over a forty-day time period to chase "sprint goals." Each man commits to reading Scripture daily, praying one brave prayer, and meeting one early morning each week for discussion and accountability. The groups are founded on the principle from Proverbs 27:17: "As iron sharpens iron, so one person sharpens another." When iron comes in contact with iron to sharpen it, it's not a gentle process. There are sparks, noise, and friction. But having gone through that process, the iron is made better and more suitable to perform its purpose.

At first I thought I was doing Joel a favor by agreeing to the early morning time slot. But I realized over time that these guys were helping our marriage. Through meeting together, they formed a bond of faith. They confessed their failures, strategized how to better love and lead, grew in devotion and faith to God, and challenged each other to become better men and husbands in the home. I happily managed breakfast duty solo with the kids for that!

Pastoral Care and Counseling

No matter how supportive your community is, there are circumstances or seasons in which these relationships cannot be a substitute for the wise counsel of pastors or counselors.

One of the most sacred parts of our jobs is when we are invited to come alongside people who want to prepare for or strengthen their marriage. Pastors and counselors are important partners in a healthy marriage.

Even if your marriage is healthy and strong, it can benefit from this support. Nathan and Heather, our neighbors who moved to the city about the same time we did and got married not long before us, impressed us around their ten-year anniversary when they told us they had committed early in their marriage to go to a counselor for a tune-up around the time of every milestone anniversary. This couple has a solid marriage, leads small groups at our church, and serves as leaders investing in marriages of other couples. But they knew outside support was an important component of their own marriage health.

At some point in your marriage, you will face a challenge that is beyond your skill set and can benefit from the support of a professional. Our friends Kristen and Jesse share openly about the healing work that counseling did in their marriage. Neither of them were screamers, and most of the conflict in their marriage seemed to develop in passive ways that weren't easy to identify. With prompting, they decided to join friends in a marriage class at church. The group counseling normalized some of the things they struggled with. As the couples in the group opened up, they began to learn healthy ways to acknowledge and grow from conflict. The class had such an impact on their marriage that they decided to pursue individual counseling. Jesse shares, "I had never done any counseling on my own, and I wasn't psyched about it. But I realized it was important."

Jesse and Kristen describe the sessions of counseling as being like peeling back layers of an onion. Layer after layer, they started to uncover the root of some things that had been festering.

They began to realize the depth of impact that some of Jesse's health issues had on the marriage. During their dating relationship, Jesse had begun to navigate some serious health complications. He was hospitalized numerous times and underwent a number of surgeries. "I knew we had committed to marriage in sickness and in health and, of course, assumed Kristen would help me through everything as my partner and advocate. There was a lot I took for granted. Through counseling, I began to understand how the severity of my illness had been somewhat of a surprise and was able to see how lonely and disappointing those first years of marriage had been for her."

Through the support of counseling, Kristen and Jesse began to reestablish the foundation of their marriage from a place of health. "We reestablished our commitment to be a team," they concluded.

Building a Support Circle

If you don't have these relationships in place, how do you start? Let's look at a few simple steps to take to build a strong circle of support.

Commit to authenticity. Invite others to be truth-tellers in your marriage. If you aren't real with yourself and others, you can't be real with God. Create an atmosphere of understanding with your community in which you will commit to be real about your shortcomings.

Make an intentional investment. Support circles require a commitment to showing up. Depth of relationship requires a certain level of sacrifice in order for you to be present in the lives of the people you care about.

Reserve judgment and expectation. A longtime friend in my life modeled a strategy she called "freedom in friendship," in which you make a conscious commitment to allow friends to live in a way you might not understand or agree with. No one cares to be in a relationship of judgment. Offer your relationships generous amounts of grace and understanding, and your circle of support will grow.

Offer grace. Make a choice to live unoffended. It's burdensome to carry offenses or disappointments. Resolve that you will assume good intentions and offer grace generously. This is the soil in which rich friendship grows.

If you and your spouse will commit to pursue these hard things, you will begin to experience the fruit of overwhelming support in your marriage.

Benefits of Community

Numerous studies testify to the health benefits of having satisfying relationships with a community of family and friends. But the benefits go beyond the physical outcomes.

Understanding and Normalization

C. S. Lewis once wrote, "Friendship, I have said, is born at the moment when one man says to another 'What! You too? I thought that no one but myself . . .'"[9]

Just as Michael and Julie learned in their small group, conversations that happen in community can normalize the issues we navigate within our own marriage. Community can also help give parameters for expectations within your marriage. Through relationships with other married couples, you can get a feel for what is common and what is perhaps outside of the boundaries of realistic expectations:

- Is it normal that you and your husband shout at each other when your emotions are high?
- Is it normal for your in-laws to stop by unannounced?
- Are your expectations of your spouse fair or excessive?
- Are other couples dealing with the same issue as you are, or is it a sign that something needs adjustment?

While you may not be asking these questions outright, spending intentional time with other couples can help you gauge the health of your marriage. A support community provides opportunities to reflect on the relationship's overall health, value, and meaningfulness.

Outside Perspective

Trusted friends can help us see things from a different perspective. One of my best friends has many of the same personality traits and tendencies Joel has. One of the gifts in our friendship is that she gives me a great deal of insight as to how Joel is processing or perceiving something in our marriage. When his response feels like a mystery to me, she can give me greater understanding about how he might be processing. I'm able to return the favor because her husband and I share some similarities. We are both external processors. Okay, we talk everything to death!

Friends can also help us adjust our expectations within

marriage. An interaction with a friend early in my marriage went like this: "I mean, he told me he had cleaned the kitchen, but then I opened the microwave and there are splatters everywhere! I mean, you didn't clean the kitchen then really, you know?" In exasperated tones, I was sharing with this friend about the cleaning negotiations in my marriage.

My friend listened and nodded. When I finished my rant, she gently pushed back.

"Hmmm. So your standard of a clean kitchen includes a clean microwave, but it seems like his does not."

"I know! Can you believe that?"

"Well, I'm just wondering why your standard is the only one that counts. I mean, if your standard is higher than his, then maybe you're the one who needs to be responsible for the difference?"

My brow furrowed. This wasn't the concurrence I had been expecting. But I was listening.

"I'm just saying that sometimes we set unfair expectations for our husbands. Then we punish them for not meeting our standards."

As frustrating as it was to not get the agreement I had been hoping for, I was grateful that my friend was willing to share another perspective. All these years later, I still think back to that dirty microwave as I realize I'm imposing my home presentation standards on Joel. That adjustment to expectations early in our marriage helped me understand that it's not fair to expect Joel to acquiesce to my every demand for domestic duties. I think I was only able to receive that perspective because it came from a trusted friend.

Shared Burden

A misconception about marriage is often a picture of two people who, once they find each other, need nothing in the world but one another. In truth, married life is much more nuanced. Joel and I have a very full life together. But one of Pastor Mark's frequent phrases rings so true: "The blessings of God complicate our lives." Our jobs, children, caring for our home, extended family, friend circles—they all require attention and focus. I can't expect Joel to be my sole counsel and support for all of that, just as I cannot be his. Since we created this life together, most of the pressures we face are shared by the other.

There is a risk of overloading marriage by asking our partner to satisfy more needs than any one individual possibly can. Friends can relieve the pressure for partners to fulfill one another's every need.

In an article titled "How to Stay Married," Stephanie Coontz, author of *Marriage, a History*, notes that "even the best-matched couples need to find gratification and support from sources other than their own partners." She cites an insight from Joshua Coleman, a therapist and author of *The Marriage Makeover*: "When they don't . . . they have less to offer each other and fewer ways to replenish their relationship. Often the marriage buckles under the weight of the partners' expectations that each will fulfill all the other's needs." Coontz agrees: "We often overload marriage by asking our partner to satisfy more needs than any one individual can possibly meet."[10]

Support for Vision

Dan and Tiffani, who are leaders in our church, have always had a vision to be a family that cares well for others. They dreamed for years of owning a home that would be a place of ministry and refuge for others. For years, Tiffani pushed through nursing school and caring for their young family, and Dan persevered through medical school and residency. The dream felt far away. They remained committed to their vision and continued to develop a strong community, investing heavily into others. They endured a painful tragedy in their family, losing Dan's brother in a tragic and devastating way, and their community offered them comfort and prayers.

This last year, they finally realized the dream of building the home they had been anticipating for so long. The night before the drywall was to be installed, they invited their large community to write prayers on the studs of the house.

Their invitation read, "We always want to be cognizant that everything we have is a gift from God and we must use what God has given us to bless others. We want our new house to be a place of refuge not only for our family but also for others. Our hope is that it will be a home base where people can leave equipped and rested."

Amazingly, the house God gave them was located on Beacon Lane, and it will serve as a beacon of hope. When people gather there, they are literally surrounded by the prayers written behind the walls around them.

Reminder and Accountability

Every relationship has seasons of difficulty when we need our support circle to remind us of the things we hold dearest. The people who know us best are best able to echo back these reminders. In his book *The Four Seasons of Marriage*, author and counselor Dr. Gary Chapman explains that every marriage goes through different seasons and some are bleaker than others. "A winter marriage," he writes, "often makes couples desperate enough to break out of their silent suffering and seek the help of a counselor, pastor, or trusted friend."[11] The summer seasons last mainly because of "the support of Christian friends and family."[12]

Dr. Chapman goes on to explain that a couple who is struggling through a winter season can benefit from the lifeline of a healthy group of friends. A couple enjoying the summer of their marriage can be that lifeline, fulfilling the call in the letter to the Hebrews: "Let us consider how to stir up one another to love and good works, not neglecting to meet together, as is the habit of some, but encouraging one another" (Hebrews 10:24–25 ESV).

God intends to use us in the lives of each other to provoke one another to love and good works. Do you have brothers and sisters in Christ who think enough of you to stir you up to love and good works?

We know a couple who spends every New Year's Day at a cabin in the mountains with other couples. They have made the commitment to one another that they will be truth-tellers in each other's marriages. They invite each other to say the hard things that others may not be willing to say. This couple says, "These friends call us back to who we are in our life stories. They have watched our life stories play out over a lot of years, and they know who we are inside that greater story. They know us well enough that they can help us remember when the narrative of life is saying something different from what we know to be true."

Henri Nouwen writes, "It is far from easy to keep living where God is. Therefore, God gives you people who help to hold you in that place and call you back to it every time you wander off."[13]

Most of our marriages suffer not for lack of desire but for lack of focus on the things we know we ought to do. Your community is a gift that God has given you to hold you accountable to who you know you are called to be.

Hebrews 13:7 tells us to follow the example of godly people. We are to not only seek their wisdom but also to pattern our life after their life. We are to "consider the outcome of their way of life and imitate their faith." Who are the couples in your life whose wisdom and life pattern you wish to emulate?

There is power in confessing to others. It brings a level of accountability to how we are living out our love. When we confess our sins to God, we are asking for forgiveness. But when we confess our sins to others, it is for healing and restoration. As James puts it, "Confess your sins to each other and pray for each other so that you may be healed. The prayer of a righteous person is powerful and effective" (James 5:16).

Prayer Support

A supportive community becomes a prayer multiplier. Every prayer investment you make as a couple can be multiplied when you have a community praying for you as well.

We saw this firsthand a few years ago. One afternoon, we got an upsetting call that our dear friends and mentors Dick and Ruth Foth were in desperate need of prayer.

Earlier that day, Ruth had slumped over in her chair during a visit with friends. She had suffered arrhythmic heart failure and was in critical condition. We were being asked to pray fervently. The depth of their circle of support became apparent as the day went on. In the same way they had poured into us for years, we were able to see just how faithfully they had been showing up in the lives of so many others.

A fierce prayer warrior, Ruth is known for lighting a candle anytime she was pressing into the Lord on someone's behalf. With that in mind, we immediately lit a candle as a reminder to pray with that same fervency. As the day went on, our social media feeds were overwhelmed by pictures of candles lit in prayer for Ruth. People were praying all over the world!

The flurry of prayers from all over the world was a testament to the relationship investments the Foths had made throughout their marriage. After thirty-six hours in a medically induced coma, Ruth woke up! Though she had suffered "sudden cardiac death," she was miraculously restored and is living a full life today.

ACTION PROMPT: Who would be the people who would overwhelm you with prayers of support when you need it the most? How are you building a community that supports your marriage in prayer? What are the ways you and your spouse support others consistently in prayer? What steps can you take to become more intentional about supporting others that way?

We see the prayers of a community at work in Acts 12. Peter had been thrown in jail for preaching the gospel. His circle of supporters immediately began to pray: "Peter was kept in prison, but the church was earnestly praying to God for him" (Acts 12:5). Though Peter was bound with chains, closely guarded, and sleeping between two soldiers, an angel woke him up, made his chains fall away, and miraculously led him out of prison unharmed. After what had happened "dawned on him, he went to the house of Mary the mother of John, also called Mark, where many people had gathered and were praying" (Acts 12:12) What a surprise it must have been to be praying earnestly and hear a knock at the door!

In reference to this passage, the Puritan preacher Thomas Watson wrote, "The angel fetched Peter out of prison, but it was prayer fetched the angel."[14] Though being in a desperate situation, Peter was rescued because of the support, the prayers, and the faith of his circle. When there was no hope for his situation, his friends spoke hope through their prayers. You will have days in your marriage when you'll seem to have no hope. Your circle can stand in that hope gap. And you will get a chance to return the favor. Stand in the gap for your circle as well. Ephesians 6:18 tells us, "Pray in the Spirit on all occasions with all kinds of prayers and requests. With this in mind, be alert and always keep on praying for all the Lord's people."

A walk through the greeting card aisle at the store will reveal the distorted views of companionship. Messages on cards read, "You complete me," or they are addressed, "To my other half." These inscriptions lay out a distorted narrative, giving us the idea that a spouse is the sole relationship we need. That is not God's design. God did not create us to be completed by one another. We are created for community, and God intends to use all of these truth-tellers, laugh givers, and generous encouragers to shape our marriage. God's perfect design for marriage includes many supporters as the circle continues to expand.

Chapter 6

Storm Circle

NINA

The recent hurricane season in our country was record-shattering and catastrophic. Fueled by abnormally warm ocean water and converging ocean patterns over the Atlantic, the season produced seventeen named storms. Ten of those storms developed into hurricanes, and six of those were classified as major hurricanes—category 3, 4, or 5.

Hurricanes Harvey, Irma, Maria, and Nate slammed into the southern coast in powerful succession. Storm after storm, powerful winds, and torrential rainfall caused destructive flooding and took out power to millions of people. Some of the greatest devastation occurred when Hurricane Maria hit Puerto Rico, claiming many lives and knocking out power to the entire island. For many months, the island suffered without electricity and basic infrastructure.

In addition to hurricanes, the United States endured other terribly destructive natural disasters in the past couple of years—wildfires, mudslides, floods, and heat waves. My own relatives were evacuated from their homes in Northern California for days when wildfires took a surprising turn toward the Sonoma County wine country, ultimately burning more than 245,000 acres and killing at least forty-three people.

Just months later, I saw my beloved college town of Montecito swept away by the mudslides that resulted from heavy rains that came in the wake of the Thomas Fire in Southern California. Unsuspecting residents and their homes were washed away when the rainfall caused a debris flow of soil that had been exposed by the fires. Families that had just returned from fire evacuation during the holidays wearily evacuated again. Awakened from sleep by the roar coming down the mountain, many lost their homes, and some lost their lives.

Ask anyone who endured any of these emergencies, and they will testify to how it became the focal point of their lives. Storms and natural disasters like these remind us how all-consuming and destructive crises can be. They demand our full attention. They refuse to allow life to carry on as is.

If it hasn't already, your marriage will face a season of storms. It will be disorienting and all-consuming, and it will stretch you personally. Some storms that couples face are fierce and surprising—the death of a child, a job loss, a life-threatening medical crisis or diagnosis. Some storms are slow-brewing and endure for a long time. They can include financial or legal hardships, a journey of infertility, a partner's mental illness, conflict with in-laws, or the pressures of caring for a child with special needs. Some marriages may endure a trial that builds over time, creating a distance between spouses due to ongoing differences of opinion or unresolved hurt. Both James and Peter warn us that we will face many kinds of trials (James 1:2; 1 Peter 1:6).

One thing about heartache is that it knows no boundaries. Adversity spins like a tornado, changing direction and taking out houses without discrimination. The longer we've been married, the more we realize that storms will hit every household.

When couples stand before their beloved on their wedding day and declare vows of commitment to one another, in their hearts each spouse truly means the words they speak. But when saying "in sickness and in health," we really are just hoping for health. When committing to stand with our spouse "for richer, for poorer," we are imagining a future that is more rich than poor.

A couple simply cannot understand the inevitable difficulties that lie ahead in marriage as they walk down the aisle; they cannot imagine feeling anything but the overwhelming love they feel at that exact moment. But anyone who has been married for long knows that the storms are certain. Sometimes they even come in succession, like Hurricanes Harvey, Irma, Maria, and Nate.

Perhaps you and your spouse are enduring trials even now. Perhaps you are grasping for hope and trying to stay afloat. Maybe you and your spouse are in a season when the waters are seemingly calm. If you haven't yet faced a trial by storm, it's inevitable that you will see that day. How can you be building a foundation to sustain you when the storm begins to rage one day?

ACTION PROMPT: Take time to reflect on the storms you've weathered as a couple. Maybe you're in the middle of a stormy season right now. How well have you weathered the storm?

Are there aftereffects you're still dealing with?

Jesus' Power Displayed in the Storm

Jesus was no stranger to storms. He used storms as a way to display His great power. The Gospels record a number of storm accounts that Jesus navigated:

> Then [Jesus] got into the boat and his disciples followed him. Suddenly a furious storm came up on the lake, so that the waves swept over the boat. But Jesus was sleeping. The disciples went and woke him, saying, "Lord, save us! We're going to drown!"
>
> He replied, "You of little faith, why are you so afraid?" Then he got up and rebuked the winds and the waves, and it was completely calm.
>
> *Matthew 8:23–26 (parallel accounts*
> *in Mark 4:36–41; Luke 8:22–25)*

When the disciples woke Jesus in a panic because of the violent storm that raged around them, He rebuked the waves and the wind, which immediately fell quiet.

All three accounts of the incident in the Gospels speak to the disciples' amazement to see this grand display of power: "Who is this? Even the wind and the waves obey him!" (Mark 4:41).

Similarly, when Peter walked on the water to Jesus, the disciples were stunned: "When they climbed into the boat, the wind died down. Then those who were in the boat worshiped him, saying, 'Truly you are the Son of God'" (Matthew 14:33).

It was only through the power Jesus displayed in the storms that His followers could see what He was capable of. As their hearts were beating fast, adrenaline pumping, they saw Jesus command power over the storm. These were pivotal points for the disciples to be able to come to a fuller understanding of Jesus' power as the Son of God.

In the same way, our difficulties allow us to see God's strength displayed in our lives. Through every weakness and hard place, we come to a greater understanding of the full power of Jesus. Of course, most of us wouldn't sign up for this kind of learning. But the scary moments bring us to a deeper humility and dependency on God that we would never have known without the trial or pain.

In the midst of your trial, God is setting you up to witness a greater expression of His power, His authority over even the wind and the waves.

PRAYER PROMPT: Ask God to use the circumstances you face as a couple as an opportunity for Him to display His power. Acknowledge and declare the authority Jesus has, even over the storms.

A Strong Foundation

When storms approach, residents in a danger zone are encouraged to shore up their property in preparation for disaster. They may cut back trees around their homes, reinforce the roof, inspect the chimney and the brickwork. If a storm is close, they will most likely board up their doors and windows in preparation.

Knowing that trials are certain in our marriage, we can take steps to build a strong foundation. You do your family a great service when you make efforts to build the foundation of marriage so it can endure a storm. God's Word tells us it's the hearing and doing of His word that builds our foundation: "Everyone then who hears these words of mine and does them will be like a wise man who built his house on the rock. And the rain fell, and the floods came, and the winds blew and beat on that house, but it did not fall, because it had been founded on the rock" (Matthew 7:24–25 ESV).

The greatest insurance is the dependence we build on the Lord. While obedience to Jesus' words is not a protection *from* the troubles, it is a protection *in* the troubles. Psalm 94:22 reads, "The LORD has become my fortress, and my God the rock in whom I take refuge."

Any builder will tell you that the time to build a strong foundation is when the sun is shining. When the sky grows dark and the rain begins to fall is not the time to build a foundation. A time of distress can come when an individual or couple tries to hurry a relationship with the Lord. You have to lay your foundation *before* a storm comes.

Joel witnessed firsthand the desolation that can come from a storm when he led a team to assist with rebuilding after a 7.3 earthquake ravaged Haiti in 2010. As bad as the quake was, shoddy construction multiplied the devastation. A report by the

Organization of American States (OAS) concluded that many of Haiti's buildings were so poorly constructed that they were unlikely to survive any disaster, let alone an earthquake of the magnitude of the one that hit Port-au-Prince: "Structures were built on slopes without proper foundations or containment structures, using improper building practices, insufficient steel and insufficient attention to development control."[1]

In fact, an earthquake in Chile just a month after the Haiti quake released five hundred times more energy than the Haiti earthquake. The death toll in Chile was in the hundreds, compared to the death toll in Haiti that was more than two hundred thousand. A huge factor was that most of the structures in Haiti were built with an improper foundation. Inadequate foundations were not identifiable until the earthquake hit. Then structure after structure collapsed in a catastrophic disaster.

PRAYER PROMPT: Ask the Lord to help you build a strong foundation that will support you and your marriage through any times of difficulty. Pray that God will reveal the areas in your marriage that can use reinforcement.

Stand on Promise

God's Word offers strong assurances of the foundation we have in Jesus. The Scriptures give us promises we can cling to in the most vulnerable times. When our marriages are being tested by trials, we must return to the promises given in God's Word.

The Promise of Growth

God's Word tells again and again that God has a plan to use the difficulties in our lives to change us. Jesus promises He is building us through the storm.

Job, who endured trials beyond measure, testified with confidence that he would come through difficulties as gold—tested, tried, and true: "He knows the way that I take; when he has tested me, I will come forth as gold" (Job 23:10). What an incredible picture of the beauty that awaits on the other side of pain!

Adam and Amy, a couple whom Joel counseled and married, experienced the transformation that comes through brokenness when they began their journey to start a family. Both Adam and Amy had come out of a broken relationship, and their finding each other felt like a miracle and the answer to their desperate prayers. "It was like God had taken these two broken people and put them back together as one thing," Amy explained.

Adam and Amy had each dreamed since childhood of having a large family. A bit older when they got married, they tried to start their family right away. The devastation of not being able to get pregnant felt like their dreams for a family were being dashed. "I wanted kids so badly. I wanted a family so badly. I was trying to trust God, but it was so painful," said Amy.

Inspired by the video of a family at church that was fostering, Adam and Amy agreed to consider a different path to parenthood. Nothing could have prepared them for the first time one of the little ones who had been placed in their care moved back home. Amy shared, "I was so happy he could be reunited with his birth family, but it felt like my heart was being ripped out.

I couldn't have known then that God was building my strength for the heartache of mothering that was still to come."

After a time, they received a little girl whose parents had been unable to care for her properly. At six months old she was malnourished, unable to sit, and barely able to hold her head up. In the midst of working to get her healthy, they got the call they had long prayed for. A baby girl needed an adoptive family. God, in His abundance, wanted them to care for *two* babies!

Caring for two baby girls at once brought its own trials. Though there have been many unexpected twists and turns in her story, the daughter they were fostering remains with Adam and Amy today. Her permanent placement is still unclear, and the uncertainty is very painful. They realize now how important it was that their faith was stretched along the way. "The Lord has been building our patience and our trust all along. He needed to write the story in a way that we knew it was from Him. For it to happen this way makes us committed to stewarding the gift of parenting these little lives, even when it's hard," said Amy.

God was also doing a refining work in the partnership of their marriage. Amy said, "Adam is such an anchor for me. He is so grounded in ways I may never be able to be. I rely on his steady resilience, and he leans into my passion to steer us forward. In our wedding vows, I told him that he is the oak tree to my hurricane. These trials are just making our roots stronger."

The Promise to Be Near

While the Scriptures testify that the trials of life are certain, one of the most consistent promises echoing throughout God's

Word is the promise that *God will be with us.* Jesus meets us in the middle of the storm.

In the middle of whatever trial you and your spouse are facing today, say it out loud to yourself: "God is with us." Declare it daily: "I am not alone. God promises to never desert me or forsake me."

The author of Hebrews records this promise of God: "Never will I leave you; never will I forsake you" (Hebrews 13:5). In Romans 8:38–39, Paul triumphantly affirms that no trial can ever separate us from the love of God.

When Jesus came walking on the water to the disciples in Matthew 14, Peter got a burst of courage:

> "Lord, if it's you," Peter replied, "tell me to come to you on the water."
>
> "Come," he said.
>
> Then Peter got down out of the boat, walked on the water and came toward Jesus. But when he saw the wind, he was afraid and, beginning to sink, cried out, "Lord, save me!"
>
> Immediately Jesus reached out his hand and caught him.
>
> *Matthew 14:28–31*

This was the same plea David made to God in Psalm 18:6:

> In my distress I called to the LORD;
> I cried to my God for help.
> From his temple he heard my voice;
> my cry came before him, into his ears . . .
> He reached down from on high and took hold of me;

> he drew me out of deep waters . . .
> He brought me out into a spacious place;
> he rescued me because he delighted in me.
>
> *Psalm 18:6, 16, 19*

Dr. Lloyd John Ogilvie was chaplain of the Senate from 1995–2003 when I started my work with Congress. He is known for saying that the prayer most certain to get God's attention is the plea, "God, help me!" Even Peter, when he stepped out of the boat and his fears began to overtake him, cried out, "Lord, save me!" And the Bible tells us, "Immediately Jesus reached out his hand and caught him." What an assurance to worship a God we know will come to our side so quickly!

Friends who pastor alongside us at National Community Church, Chris and Kathryn, felt the power of God's presence when they cried out to him in the darkest time. Their perfect storm hit just a few years into their marriage in a season that was supposed to be a time of blessing. One night in October 2016, Chris came home from work to find Kathryn waiting with news. After trying for almost a year, they were pregnant. More surprises followed when at their first doctor appointment they learned that Kathryn was carrying twin girls!

They had barely adjusted to the shock when at their seventeen-week appointment the doctor saw something that caused concern. While baby A was growing normally, baby B's heart didn't seem to be formed exactly right. The doctor quickly scheduled them for a fetal echocardiogram the following week, just before Christmas.

The fetal echo brought a difficult report. Baby B had a

congenital heart defect called hypoplastic left heart syndrome. Put simply, she had just one side of her heart, the right atrium and right ventricle, while the left ventricle and atrium had never formed. Baby B would require a series of surgeries soon after her birth and into the first few years of her life.

Chris and Kathryn and their friends and family were devastated, but they prayed through the remaining weeks of pregnancy, and on May 1, 2017, at 4:15 p.m., Ryan Grace and Keelyn Joy were born. Their sweet faces were a gift in a season that had been filled with so much trial.

Little Keelyn was transferred to the nearby children's hospital and grew sick faster than anyone expected. Just a couple of days after Keelyn's birth, her parents were in her room for a visit when alarms in the room began to sound. Within moments, the room was filled with nursing staff, who started to do bag mask ventilation on the tiny baby. A nurse began chest compressions, and Chris and Kathryn were rushed into the waiting room next door.

Chris describes the peace that filled the waiting room in the midst of chaos: "The room became light and weightless, as though we had actually hit the eye of the hurricane. I could sense that it was the peace of God that passes all understanding. In that moment, I didn't know if that peace meant my daughter was alive or dead. But I could sense with certainty that, regardless of the outcome, it was going to be okay. I felt overwhelming assurance that God was good and would not waver in the storm."

Chris and Kathryn testify to how close the Lord felt in those days. They would need him even more in the days ahead. Keelyn was stabilized that day, but over the course of the next few months, she would undergo numerous surgeries in an attempt to repair her heart. The storm raged again months later when tests showed that Keelyn had pulmonary vein stenosis and intervention options were becoming more limited.

For months, our church family circled the family with meal trains, babysitting assistance, and persistent prayers. Keelyn's team of doctors continued to brainstorm all options to repair her heart. But the time came when the doctors delivered the grave news: Keelyn's organs were shutting down. Just seven months into their little daughter's life, Chris and Kathryn had to say good-bye. There are moments in ministry when there's just nothing you can say to make it better. We had no words. Yet the presence of the Lord that came so powerfully those first few days would be strikingly present through it all. Chris and Kathryn's strong faith held them steady in that deeply painful time. Their commitment to one another has been a stable foundation through the days that have followed.

PRAYER PROMPT: In the midst of your trial, call out to the Lord, "Help me!" Ask Him to draw near to you and your spouse and to allow you to feel Him close. Ask Him to use the trial to unify you and your spouse.

The Promise of a Greater Good

As a great Redeemer, God can be trusted to not waste our pain. Romans 8:28 assures us that "in all things God works for the good of those who love him, who have been called according to his purpose." That is not a trite promise!

John 16:33 echoes a similar promise of victory: "I have told you these things, so that in me you may have peace. In this world you will have trouble. But take heart! I have overcome the world." While there will be trouble in the world, Jesus has already overcome it!

Chris and Kathryn find great comfort that their little Keelyn's life, while short, was an incredible blessing to so many people. Her life is a reminder that true victory is beyond this world.

Adam and Amy have confidence that, though their parenting story is being written differently from what they imagined, God is working a great purpose through their family.

The apostle Paul writes these words: "Though outwardly we are wasting away, yet inwardly we are being renewed day by day. For our light and momentary troubles are achieving for us an eternal glory that far outweighs them all. So we fix our eyes not on what is seen, but on what is unseen, for what is seen is temporary, but what is unseen is eternal" (2 Corinthians 4:16–18).

Survival Protocol

Because of where we live in Washington, D.C., we have friends who are positioned in critical decision-making positions when our country faces danger. A longtime friend of ours served at the White House as the senior director for resilience policy during the many disasters that recently faced our nation. He shared with us the way decisions are made during emergencies. He told us that priority in a crisis situation always goes to the things that are life-saving and life-sustaining. Every other priority falls underneath those. In those moments, nothing else can be equally important because resources are limited.

This is important advice for the difficulties we will face in our marriages. During a time of crisis or testing, all priorities must adjust to the things that will save us. A return to the spiritual disciplines, the basics of our faith, will keep us aligned with the Lord during the most disorienting times. In times of turbulence, returning to those basics of our relationship with the Lord and with our spouses will keep us strong and our marriages enduring. It is a survival protocol for our marriage.

No one understands the importance of protocol more than the men and women who serve our nation. Because of the dangers they face, our military has a deep understanding that in times of desperation, they must return to frequently practiced basic procedures to ensure safety or to shore up against a threat.

Because Washington, D.C., is a decision-making center for our country, we have many military personnel from all branches who attend our church. The National Community Church location where we pastor is just across the street from the oldest post in the United States Marine Corps. Established in 1801, it remains the official residence of the commandant of the Marine Corps and is the main ceremonial grounds of the Corps. We are just one block from the United States Navy Yard, the oldest shore establishment of the U.S. Navy, which serves as their ceremonial and administrative grounds.

One of our dearest friends in D.C. is a rear admiral in the United States Coast Guard. To ensure that they are prepared to conduct operational missions, Coast Guard units maintain the highest readiness standards. In the face of storms or dangers while on a ship, you focus on the basic shipboard functions that give you the greatest chance of survival.

Batten Down the Hatches

The early-nineteenth-century nautical term "batten down the hatches" is a warning that sailors called out when a storm was on its way. The square or rectangular holes in the deck of the ships were called hatches or hatchways. They are used to load cargo into a ship's interior or hold. One might also climb through the hatches to get to the living quarters below deck. In old sailing ships, hatches were covered with an open wooden grate. These grates prevented sailors from falling through the hatches as they walked across the deck and also let fresh air and sunlight flow down to the ship's lower decks.

Battens were long wooden sticks used to attach canvas to a ship's hatches, covering them in the face of an approaching storm. If water crashed over the bow of the ship and ran across the deck and down into the hatches, the ship could fill with water and potentially sink. To prevent this, deckhands battened down the hatches, covering them with canvas.

In anticipation of the trials that will confront your marriage, it's wise to make sure you have not neglected the most vital practices that will sustain you and give you the greatest chance for survival. Practicing the spiritual disciplines is a way to "batten down the hatches" against a storm that is brewing. Faith disciplines ensure a strong foundation for our faith and for our marriages. They are survival protocols, a way to "shore up" our house.

Scripture study, prayer, gratitude, service, fasting—when our marriages begin to endure a trial, it will be these spiritual disciplines that stabilize us. They are the power to the most vital circuits.

Of course, it is our belief that one of the surest ways to build a strong foundation is prayer. The premise of this book is that a foundation of prayer in your marriage is what will keep you connected to the Lord and also to one another. We hope you will make a new commitment to daily prayer over your marriage and anything it will endure. Set a time each day that is committed to prayer. Set a rhythm to pray with your spouse. Write your prayers in a journal. Make your prayers a mantra that you echo to the Lord each day.

God's Word calls us to "pray without ceasing" (1 Thessalonians 5:17 ESV), and this means we must return our thoughts to Him again and again. In one of my favorite stories about the way we have to train our minds to connect with the Lord, Father Thomas Keating, a priest and teacher of contemplative prayer, shares about a workshop in which a nun lamented after making her first attempt at extended prayer, "Oh, Father Thomas, I'm such a failure at this prayer. In twenty minutes I've had ten thousand thoughts!" Father Keating responded without missing a beat, "How lovely! You returned your thoughts to God ten thousand times!"[2] Keating affirmed that praying without ceasing is about bringing our mind back to the Lord again and again. It is that continual conversation with the Lord that will provide a steady foundation of peace in the most difficult times.

One misconception we have is that prayer is simply a one-way conversation to the Lord. Prayer is just as much about listening and allowing God's Spirit to speak to you, to comfort you, to lead you. A friend described to me once that it is through prayer that the things of the world fall away and the things of the Lord rise. I think of that often when I'm in the midst of difficulty. As I return to the Lord again and again in prayer and reflection, the thoughts and feelings that are mine begin to fall away over time, and His leading begins to rise to the surface and bring me clarity.

Let's look at a few reminders of things that can strengthen a marriage in times of difficulty.

Remember Better Times

There's a wealth of research showing that people with chronic illness such as cancer, AIDS, and type 2 diabetes can live longer if they demonstrate a positive outlook. And there's also evidence that a focus on better times can keep a marriage healthy during difficulty. Research by Dr. John Gottman, one of the world's leaders in marriage research, points to studies indicating that couples who remain mindful of the relationship's best moments are able to strengthen their commitment during the hardest times.[3] Gottman recommends that a couple reminisce about better days, such as how they met, memories from dating, the wedding day, happy times with their children, and the amazing blessings from God. The research shows that dreaming together about what they want to do when the difficult time passes is an encouraging way to remind a couple that they are in it together. Dream together about what you want to do when this storm passes.

Many of the couples we talked to about how they navigate their most painful moments have shared the importance of seeing themselves as a team. Many of them noted a significant moment in their journey when they made a decision out loud to one another to be unified as a team, no matter the circumstance.

God's promise in our trials is that they will provide growth and a deeper understanding and commitment. When we are in the midst of a storm, it's easy to allow uncertainty, pain, and plans to overtake our marriage. Sometimes storms can last for months or even years. Unless we act to prevent it, the emotions from the storm will become the new culture in our home. The only escape is to be deliberate in our determination to avoid this.

Share funny family stories to remind your spouse of God's faithfulness to you throughout your lives. Compliment one another. Make it a habit to remind your spouse of your unswerving commitment to them. Tell your mate how happy you are to have them in your life.

Keep the trial from overtaking you by creating trouble-free time together. Create lighthearted moments by finding ways to call out things that will bring laughter. The book of Proverbs reminds us that "a cheerful heart is good medicine" (Proverbs 17:22). Nehemiah 8:10 tells us that "the joy of the LORD is your strength."

Wise Counsel

Every storm leaves damage that needs attention to keep it from causing lasting deterioration. One of my greatest prayers over marriages has been that God will do a healing work to keep small fissures from developing into fractures that are harder to repair.

This is even more important during vulnerable times. Depending solely on your spouse to process and asking for their support in carrying your burdens when they're also walking through the trial is unfair. Invite others to walk alongside you.

Depending on the severity of the crisis, professional counsel may be warranted. Counselors are trained to be a listening ear and offer feedback, and they can point out things a couple may not otherwise see.

Weather the Storm

Couples who have endured the most difficult trauma attest that in the darkest part of the storm it was nothing more than sheer commitment that kept their marriage intact.

At some point, when the storm has raged to its greatest intensity, a covenant perspective may be the last line of defense. Most couples who have endured trial share that there was at least one point where the only thing that kept them from separating was the resolve that marriage is a forever commitment. Their enduring commitment became the saving grace of the marriage.

Psychologists at the Relationship Institute at UCLA have conducted research that shows the importance of a certain level of resolve in order to preserve a relationship. The psychologists studied 172 married couples over the first eleven years of marriage. They found that couples who displayed a commitment to preserving the marriage and were willing to make sacrifices within their relationships were more likely to have lasting and happy marriages. The codirector of the Relationship Institute, Thomas Bradbury, said, "What our data indicate is that committing to the relationship rather than committing to your own agenda and your own immediate needs is a far better strategy."[4]

We tend to view marriage through a consumer mind-set. Sociologists argue that in Western society, we are so affected by the marketplace mentality that we even approach relationships as consumers. Individual happiness has become the ultimate value. We engage in a relationship as long as it's meeting our needs at a cost we are willing to accept. When it requires more from us than we are getting back, we move on.

Mexico City considered a plan in 2011 (which didn't pass) that would introduce "temporary marriage licenses." The marriage license would expire after two years. At that time, you would just split or you'd decide to renew your marriage and continue on. The assemblyman who coauthored the bill said, "The proposal is, when the two-year period is up, if the relationship is not stable or harmonious, the contract simply ends."[5] This proposal offered a voidable agreement that is dissolved if the two parties don't like its course. This process by which social relationships are reduced to economic exchange effectively reduces a sacred relationship to a simple contract.

The biblical understanding of marriage presents marriage as a covenant. Covenant is not practiced when you feel like it. It is not abandoned in the midst of trial. It's not convenient, suitable, or easy. Rather, it is involved, committed, and relational.

It is the kind of commitment that promises to endure through any kind of storm. It is the kind of love that requires a high level of sacrifice. Jesus was the perfect example of this perfect sacrifice. The Scriptures tell us we love because God first loved us (1 John 4:19). It is leaning into that perfect love that helps us live out our promise.

During the hardest times, the raw commitment you swore when you made your vows may be the only thing that keeps you hanging on. The fact that—way back when—you said "till death do us part" may be the only reason you keep two feet in long enough to fix what's not going well. And that is reason enough.

Marriage is about the transformation of our hearts to be more like God. This is our pursuit. Happiness, satisfaction, emotional well-being, and contentment are all by-products of a healthy marriage. They are secondary results, not the main pursuit. It is our desire for God, more than our desire for our spouse, that should empower us to live out this covenant in the toughest times.

Circle the Trial in Faith

Faith is the currency of the kingdom of God. Somehow God's supernatural power seems to move most through faith-filled people. Faith without a profession of God's ability is nothing more than wishful thinking. Calling out to the Lord as we stand on His promises is the way we maintain our focus on Jesus rather than on the storm.

God desires to use our marriages so we might offer one another the strength to overcome. We can help each other as navigators through rough waters. Pastor Mark often reminds our church to "stop speaking to God about your problems and start speaking to your problems about God." We serve a God who is able to overcome. We need to declare that today.

PRAYER PROMPT: In response to the trials you and your spouse are enduring, pray this declaration of God's Word over your situation. Use God's Word to anchor your marriage in any storm.

Prayer of Declaration

Father, Your Word reminds us that You are with us through the most difficult times. Help us to see You as the stronghold for our marriage through rough waters. Give us confidence that we can rely on You.

Psalm 46:1–2: "God is our refuge and strength, an ever-present help in trouble. Therefore we will not fear."

• • • • • •

Lord, You promise to never leave us or forsake us. Come into our marriage and help us to feel Your presence.

Matthew 28:20: "Surely I am with you always, to the very end of the age."

. . . . . .

Thank You, Lord, that we can declare Your victory over every problem or difficulty. Thank You for giving us to each other in marriage to offer strength and support to one another. Give us peace in Your larger plan.

John 16:33: "I have told you these things, so that in me you may have peace. In this world you will have trouble. But take heart! I have overcome the world."

. . . . . .

Lord, we choose to set our minds and hearts on You rather than the troubles we face. Give us an eternal perspective of the work You are doing.

2 Corinthians 4:18: "We fix our eyes not on what is seen, but on what is unseen, since what is seen is temporary, but what is unseen is eternal."

. . . . . .

Thank You that You are our trusted Redeemer and that You will never waste our pain. Help us to trust in the greater good You are working through our trials.

Romans 8:28: "We know that in all things God works for the good of those who love him, who have been called according to his purpose."

. . . . . .

Lord, we surrender to the way You use our circumstances to develop us. Use every trial to strengthen the depth of our commitment to one another. Give us joy in the obstacles we are overcoming.

James 1:2–3: "Consider it pure joy, my brothers and sisters, whenever you face trials of many kinds, because you know that the testing of your faith produces perseverance."

• • • • • •

Though our marriage may feel weak or unsteady, we trust that we can depend on Your steadfast strength. You are our Helper, and all things are possible through You.

2 Corinthians 12:9–10: "[The Lord] said to me, "My grace is sufficient for you, for my power is made perfect in weakness. Therefore I will boast all the more gladly about my weaknesses, so that Christ's power may rest on me. That is why, for Christ's sake, I delight in weaknesses, in insults, in hardships, in persecutions, in difficulties. For when I am weak, then I am strong."

• • • • • •

We acknowledge that You are our Protector. You promise to go before us and also to cover us from behind. We commit to reminding our spouse to trust in Your power and protection.

Isaiah 52:12: "The LORD will go before you, the God of Israel will be your rear guard."

Chapter 7

Legacy Circle

JOEL

One spring day while on a walk, Honi the circle maker noticed a very old man planting a carob tree. Honi asked, "Excuse me, sir, but how long does it take for this tree to bear fruit?" The man replied, "In about seventy years, this tree will produce carobs good enough for eating." "Do you think you will live seventy more years and be able to eat the carob fruit?" asked Honi. The man replied, "Oh no! But I remember enjoying carob fruits as a young boy from trees planted by those who wanted to leave a gift for younger people. Just as my parents and grandparents planted trees for me, so I plant trees for my children and grandchildren."[1]

The story of Honi the circle maker is a story about bold prayers and a bold God who honors them. But this second story about Honi shows a defining moment for the scholar.

The day Honi drew the circle and prayed for rain, he taught

rabbis about great faith in God. In this lesser-known legend, Honi becomes the student. Honi couldn't understand why a man would plant a tree he wouldn't be able to eat the fruit from. He thought the point of planting was the personal enjoyment of it. So to his way of thinking, an inability to see and to eat the fruit made the planting a pointless endeavor. Honi's perspective was shortsighted and self-centered.

But the planter of the tree was a dreamer. He understood the previous generations' sacrifice for him. And he understood a long view of legacy. His actions, though not helpful to him personally, would be an investment into many generations beyond his life.

We think that what God does for us is just for us. No! What God does for us is also for the third and fourth generations. God is always thinking bigger and longer than we are.

We desire a good marriage because we want the fruit of a good marriage. But a deeper grasp of the idea of covenant is to seek fruit that future generations will receive.

Jonathan Edwards is known for his powerful thirty-two-page treatise titled "Sinners in the Hands of an Angry God," but he has a remarkable résumé of accomplishments, including his sermons, his books, and his service as president of Princeton University. He was a principal influence in the Great Awakening of the 1700s.

But his personal résumé is dwarfed by his marital impact. He and his wife, Sarah, had eleven children together and were deeply committed and intertwined with one another. They were partners in ministry who worked together on church challenges and the crafting of sermons. They counted on each other and spent time communicating around their goals. Once their kids got old enough, they included them in their discussions about theology.

The marriage of Jonathan and Sarah Edwards had a multiplication impact on generations to follow. As Mark Batterson notes in his book *Draw the Circle*, "Of his known descendants there are more than 300 ministers or missionaries, 120 university professors, 60 authors, 30 judges, 14 college presidents, 3 members of Congress, and 1 vice president."[2]

The spiritual legacy of a marriage began to build when the couple started to realize their relationship was so much bigger than themselves. When a couple steps into that unique marriage print that God designed, the legacy begins to be realized. Death to self means life to the Spirit. Jonathan Edwards acknowledged this on January 12, 1723, when he surrendered himself to the Lord. He issued this dedication: "I made a solemn dedication of myself to God, and wrote it down; giving up myself, and all that I had to God; to be for the future, in no respect, my own; to act as one that had no right to himself, in any respect. And solemnly vowed, to take God for my whole portion and felicity; looking on nothing else, as any part of my happiness, nor acting as if it were."[3]

The Edwards's marriage print echoed not just to the next generation. It reverberated throughout our country's history and has had an exponential impact on many sectors of society.

PRAYER PROMPT: Pause and say a simple prayer that God will give you inspiration as you read this chapter. Ask the Lord to help you plant for future generations and birth a legacy from your marriage.

Cultivating a legacy in my own family, my great-grandfather Christian Schmidgall arrived on Ellis Island on May 17, 1902. Sixteen years old, he had only ten dollars to his name and didn't speak English. Somehow he made his way to central Illinois, doing a few odd jobs to make ends meet. There he rented a farm and eventually bought eighty acres. That eighty acres is now farmed by my cousins, his great-grandsons. Though Christian farmed oats and hay, the fields are now filled with beans and corn. This past summer, we took our family back to Illinois to celebrate the anniversary of the church my parents started fifty years ago. We took the opportunity to take my kids to the farm in rural Illinois and let them run through the bean fields.

I was struck by the generational impact that my great-grandfather has had. I think it's fair to say that the seed planted by Christian Schmidgall a hundred years ago is still reaping a harvest to the third and fourth generations.

I'm not sure if Christian Schmidgall was thinking so far into the future, but God was. He is the God of generations. He is the God of Abraham, the God of Isaac, and the God of Jacob.

In the 1940s when Christian Schmidgall put his faith in Jesus Christ, God became the God of Christian and then the God of Edgar and then the God of Bob and then the God of Joel and now the God of my children. My great-grandfather made a decision he thought affected just him, but it was a multiple-generation decision, and hopefully for many more to come! Your faith has far more impact than you can imagine. We think right here, right now, but God is thinking nations and generations. As the apostle Peter said in his Pentecost address, "The promise is for you and your children and for all who are far off—for all whom the Lord our God will call" (Acts 2:39).

Your marriage, your decisions, will have a generational impact. Do you realize the impact of your actions? And do you acknowledge the impact of the actions of those who came before you? Your life is a result of the prayers of those who have come before you. And future generations, good or bad, will be the result of the prayers you pray, the life you live, the consecration you make, the vision you live out today.

Legacy of Sacrifice

In chapter 2, Nina and I outlined the vision we've wrestled with in prayer. Our marriage print is unique to our marriage. However, it doesn't stand alone. Our vision is the result of values that were lived out and prayed forward from generations before us. There were seeds planted years ago that began to sprout when we said, "I do."

Our commitment to service and sacrifice and "giving more than we receive" was planted years before our own marriage started. When I was a kid, each year our family gave to support missional efforts around the world. We financially contributed to those who were serving people in need and sharing faith in Christ with the spiritually poor. My parents held the conviction that it was our responsibility to support those who had left a life of comfort to live in other nations and incarnate a message of hope.

One year, my parents prayed about what to give and felt prompted to pledge the entire value of their home toward the church's efforts. My father was the pastor of our church, and as I look back, I think it would've been so encouraging for a community of people to see their leader put his money where his heart was. But as a child of those parents, it was horrible news! It's the reason we never got the name-brand items! Instead we got Bran with Raisins, Fruity Rings, Flakes That Are Frosted, and if it was a good week, maybe some Dr. Thunder to drink. Popsicles were leftover juice in the ice cube tray with toothpicks. We didn't play Nintendo; we played the Un-Game. It was cards with questions. That was the game. You couldn't even win! My sister used to say it's called the Un-Game because it takes the "F" out of Fun.

If that wasn't bad enough, our parents challenged us kids to give to missions too. We called it a faith promise. "Now, kids, you don't have to give, but here's a pledge card and a pen, but of course it's under your own volition." My father stood over us as we filled it out. "Here you go, Dad." Father would frown with a discontented look. "Oh, yeah, Dad, I uh, forgot a 0. It should've been $100." "That's better, Joel. You're seven years old now." Okay, I might've exaggerated that one.

This wasn't a one-time thing. We had faith promise every six months. Every time I turned around, I was asked for missions dollars. *I just emptied out my wallet for that guy from Mozambique; now here comes another missionary.* I couldn't keep up with my mission debt. I had to start selling drugs just to support my missions-giving habit. Okay, I definitely exaggerated that time!

Because my parents had a vision in their own marriage and lived it, my siblings and I had a front-row seat to the testimony of a God-honoring relationship. And every single one of us had a seed planted in our hearts. Their legacy was birthed in us.

Nina's family also shared a commitment to putting others first. Nina can recite countless times when her parents made sacrifices to care for another. It happened so regularly that Nina started to tease her parents, asking if someone had painted a red cross on their front door.

One summer, Nina's family skipped a vacation because a friend needed to borrow funds to keep the electricity on in their home. Her parents handed over their vacation funds without question, and they did something in their local area instead.

During her high school years, it wasn't rare for Nina to get up to leave for school and find a family friend sleeping on the couch. This friend had received a citation for driving under the influence of alcohol, and Nina's parents told him that, for his own safety, if he ever had a few drinks, they wanted him to stay at their house rather than drive to his house in the next town.

Nina's dad befriended a blind man who worked in the darkroom of the X-ray lab at the same hospital. When Dad learned that Jim spent many holidays alone, he became a regular at their Thanksgiving table and family outings to the sporting events he loved.

Though Nina's dad sported a ponytail he was very proud of, he cut it off and shaved his head in solidarity with a coworker who was undergoing cancer treatments. Even animals were welcomed with loving arms. There wasn't a stray cat or dog that wasn't fed or cared for if it wandered into their yard.

A legacy is not made by what you get; it's made by what you give. Nina and I both received an inheritance of self-sacrifice. We have every intention of passing along that same inheritance to our own children and to the people in our community.

Renewed Legacy

Don't underestimate the echo of your covenant. According to a study by Dr. Tim Clinton, only five out of one hundred spouses interviewed desired a marriage that replicates their parents.[4] There are generations that have been handed a legacy of marriage that is counterfeit to what God desires. Perhaps you were handed a distorted version of marriage. Maybe your parents had a marriage where denial was the ruling emotion or their marriage was built on a codependency that was anything but life-giving. Maybe one of your parents dominated decisions and always got their way. Maybe your parents went through an ugly divorce. It can be discouraging to face up to the shortcomings in the legacy we inherited.

Perhaps you're even doing some things that are passing along a distorted vision of marriage to others. It's overwhelming to confront the areas where we fall short of the best that God intends for our marriages and our families. Even now, I feel convicted that I'm not passing on a better version of covenant love to our children, friends, and the young people in our lives. We have to put fear, discouragement, and apathy to death. Daily. That starts by confessing our failures to God. The Bible teaches that "if we confess our sins, [God] is faithful and just and will forgive us our sins and purify us from all unrighteousness" (1 John 1:9).

The next step is to confess our faults to those in our lives. James 5:16 reads, "Therefore confess your sins to each other and pray for each other so that you may be healed."

As Nina shared in chapter 6, when we confess our sins to God, we are asking for forgiveness. But when we confess our sins to others, it is meant for healing and restoration. I have seen my wife faithfully give grace when I simply ask for forgiveness. I have found my kids to be amazingly resilient when I confess my mistakes to them. Once you've confessed, do not linger in your mistakes. Refocus on living out a legacy.

The apostle Paul writes, "There is now no condemnation for those who are in Christ Jesus, because through Christ Jesus the law of the Spirit who gives life has set you free from the law of sin and death" (Romans 8:1–2). Stop condemning yourself. There is a time when you must let go of your mistakes and start walking out the purpose God placed in you before you were even born. Here's how we say it at National Community Church: "It's never too late to be who you might have been."

I love the old story of a man named Alfred. As the story goes, a rich and successful man had picked up a French newspaper to read his brother's obituary. Instead, he read his own obituary! The editor had accidentally mixed up the two brothers. The headline proclaimed, "The Merchant of Death Is Dead." The article described a man who gained his wealth by helping people kill one another. Together he and his father and brother had invented dynamite to be used for construction purposes. Alfred was deeply disturbed at this glimpse of his legacy. It's believed that this pivotal experience was the reason he left the majority of his fortune to those whose work most benefited humanity. Today the world knows him as Alfred Nobel, the founder of the Nobel Prize.[5]

PRAYER PROMPT: Romans 3:23 reads, "All have sinned and fall short of the glory of God." How have you fallen short and allowed hang-ups to stunt what God wants to accomplish in and through you? Ask God to help you commit to a new legacy going forward.

Take a Posture of Prayer

A number of years ago, I was in a season where I was faithfully seeking God for a vision for our kids. Right in the middle of that season, our church held an all-night prayer meeting. It was twelve hours straight of prayer and worship. I committed that night to taking a Jacob posture of prayer.

In Genesis 32, Jacob had come upon the river Jabbok, where he met a man believed to be an angel. Jacob, desperate for a blessing, wrestled him the entire night and refused to let go until he received a blessing (Genesis 32:22–26). It showed not only Jacob's fortitude but also his determination to redirect his life and legacy. It was that night that Jacob shifted from his own plans to God's priorities. It was the birth of his legacy. His name was changed from Jacob, meaning "he deceives," to Israel—"one who struggles with God." He named that place Peniel ("face of God"), because he saw God face to face (Genesis 32:30).

With the same determination, I resolved that night that I would wrestle in prayer all night to grasp a blessing for my kids. I was praying for a picture of legacy.

Not surprisingly, it's hard to pray for that long! But there is something irreplaceable about depth of prayer. There is a connection to the Lord that you can receive only through persistence. It's similar to a second wind or the endorphin rush you can get as a runner. It was around 2 a.m. when I finally had a breakthrough. I got a picture of the potential for the future of my three kids. I began to thank God in prayer for the beautiful picture of what could be. Then I asked a question in prayer: "Lord, how can I help?" Ha! When you seek God for a vision, you don't realize you're actually asking God to give you a big task that will require sacrifice and growth! Following the vision came this conviction from the Lord in prayer. It was the inaudible but unmistakable voice of God: *Whatever you want your kids to be in eighteen years, you have to be that* now.

I heard the message loud and clear. If I wanted my kids to be worshipers, I had to be a worshiper now. If I wanted my kids to have a spirit of generosity, I had to be generous now. Whatever I wanted to see, I had to be. It was a revelation that has altered the way I see myself before God and before my family. It's a core value, a deep conviction that I have to *live* out.

As I prayed that my kids would be grace givers, I was faced with my failures to give grace in my own home. As I prayed that my kids would take bold actions of love toward others, I became acutely aware that I was not taking those bold actions myself. I was convicted to change, and I began to live out grace, boldness, love, patience, and faith in a more tangible and intentional way. I had to live it to give it!

The phrase "upstream reciprocity" is used to describe the multiplying effect our actions can have on others. Similar to the concept of paying it forward, this effect occurs when an act of altruism causes the recipient to perform a later act for the benefit of another.

An act of kindness can have a physical effect on people. In fact, a release of endorphins and serotonin happens in both the receiver and the giver. Allan Luks, former executive director of the Institute for the Advancement of Health, states, "A rush of euphoria, followed by a longer period of calm, after performing a kind act is often referred to as a 'helper's high.' It involves physical sensations and the release of endorphins, the body's natural painkillers."[6]

Danica Collins takes it a step further in her article titled "The Act of Kindness and Its Positive Health Benefits": "What's even more amazing is that persons observing the act of kindness also experience a similar strengthening of the immune system and increased production of serotonin! Kindness is a win-win-win scenario which produces beneficial effects in the giver, the recipient and the observer."[7]

In other words, a loving marriage will have a ripple effect. When a couple draws a circle around their marriage and cultivates their marriage print and puts it into practice, it's like the classic example of throwing a stone in the water. The initial splash produces one small ring, hardly bigger than the stone itself. But then it grows bigger and bigger. A multiplication happens, and new rings begin to spread outward in concentric circles. It's almost like you're watching generations of one rock. There are generations of your grace and a legacy of your love. What or who are the generations of your marriage?

Maturity helps us to understand that marriage is not just about you or your spouse, your kids, or your friends. It's about friends of friends, neighbors, grandchildren, and people with whom you may have no contact but who will be beneficiaries of the work God is doing in and through your marriage. Your inspiration will reach people that your actions won't. It's not just about your accomplishments, but about what you inspire in others.

PRAYER PROMPT: Ask God to give you a grander vision, a longer view, and a fuller understanding of the legacy of your actions. Ask Him to help you understand that the oak tree of a next generation is the seed of your prayer life today.

Portfolio of Investment

Each year, when Nina and I take our annual vision retreat, we spend a significant amount of time on our portfolio of investments. I'm not talking about mutual funds or a 401(k) or money invested in stocks or real estate. We're not concerned with how much money we are making, but with how much of our resources we are investing. We spend a significant amount of time evaluating portfolio categories like relationships, neighborhood, missions, church community, family, and children. To ensure that we stay focused on our spiritual legacy, we must continually remind ourselves of our marriage vision: *to give more than we receive*. This means we need to be giving more of our time, our talents, our home, and our energy to others than we expect in return. We focus less on accumulation of wealth and more on investing in life. It's a simple transition of focus. We shift the focus from *what* is our legacy to *who* is our legacy.

Whom are you investing in as a couple? If you sit down with a financial adviser, they almost always counsel you to diversify your portfolio. There's richness that comes when you spread your finances across different types of stocks, bonds, and funds. Utilize the same principle when you think about the who of your legacy. Have you diversified your portfolio? Do you only hang out with people who look and act like you? Here are some questions we ask to help diversify our relational portfolio:

- What couples are we investing in?
- Who are we learning from?
- What friendships are we building with single people?
- What relationships do we have with people who are older and younger than us?
- How are we crossing lines of division in relationships (ethnicity, faith, socioeconomic class, and so forth)?

Pleasing or Purposeful

When Nina and I realized that marriage is bigger than us, it helped us understand that our relationship is less about our gratification and more about God's glory. Are you aiming for a pleasing marriage or a purposeful marriage? Our tendency is to hyperfocus on the personal happiness we can get out of our relationships.

In her book *The Power of Meaning*, psychologist Emily Esfahani Smith writes, "Indeed social scientists have uncovered a sad irony—chasing happiness actually makes people unhappy."[8] She cites a 2013 study by a team of psychologists from Florida State that revealed that happiness and meaning are often at odds.

The pursuit of happiness was linked to selfish behavior. But contributing to something beyond one's self was the defining feature in leading to meaningful life.[9] She quotes the conclusion of three psychologists—Richard Ryan, Veronika Huta, and Edward Deci: "The more directly one aims to maximize pleasure and avoid pain, the more likely one is to produce, instead, a life bereft of depth, meaning, and community."[10]

Pastor Andy Stanley puts it this way: "If you live for yourself, lead for yourself, in the end you will have nothing to show for yourself but yourself."[11] Marriage by design is meant to produce. In fact, it was God's first mandate to mankind: "God blessed them and said to them, 'Be fruitful and multiply'" (Genesis 1:28 NLT). And some would argue that it's the only command mankind has truly kept. But what is it that God blesses us for? For happiness? To please the couple? No, He blesses them and *gives them purpose*.

25 Cents at a Time

Vision can be born in a moment in a prayer closet, but legacy is built day by day throughout life. Every day in which you live out your vision in your marriage is like putting a brick on the house of legacy.

Former Emory University theology professor Fred Craddock described living a kingdom life on earth like this:

> To give my life for Christ appears glorious . . . We think giving our all to the Lord is like taking a $1,000 bill and laying it on the table—"Here's my life, Lord. I'm giving it all."
>
> But the reality for most of us is that he sends us to the bank and has us cash in the $1,000 for quarters. We go

through life putting out 25 cents here and 50 cents there. Listen to the neighbor kid's troubles instead of saying, "Get lost." Go to a committee meeting. Give a cup of water to a shaky old man in a nursing home.

Usually giving our life to Christ isn't glorious. It's done in all those little acts of love, 25 cents at a time. It would be easy to go out in a flash of glory; it's harder to live the Christian life little by little over the long haul.[12]

There's a well-known practice called the obituary exercise that can help you think about your legacy with the end in mind. The exercise forces you to imagine being at your funeral so that you can identify the values, stories, and people you hope to have as your legacy. I want to encourage you to slow down your reading and practice a variation of this as a relational exercise.

Picture yourself walking into your favorite eatery where tables have been set up for a fiftieth wedding anniversary party. You and your spouse walk into the room filled with people you know. And as you look at the picture and name that are set up on an easel, you realize the party is for you. I want to ask you to take a moment to answer the following questions:

- Who is in attendance?
- What are the stories that people tell about your marriage?
- How do people explain each spouse's uniqueness and how it fits together in the relationship?
- What are the difficult parts of your marriage that have stood out to others? What hurdles have they seen you overcome together?

- What do people say you did for each other or for them?
- What is the one-sentence description at the top of the program that captures the legacy of your marriage?
- If your spouse had to write down the memories and things they appreciated about you, what would they say?

Perhaps you hope your friends will describe you as someone who puts your spouse ahead of yourself, who pulls the best out of them, who honors them behind their back. You may hope your children remember the moments when things went awry on vacation and you made the best of it. Or that they'd share about the time one of you lost your job and both of you pulled together in a way that made your relational roots much deeper. Maybe your spouse will share about how you made them laugh in good and tough times or how you set work aside to put their needs first or how you do the little things nobody else knows about that show love or how you just make them better.

I hope my wife will say I'm a steady and faithful force for her. I hope she'll remember me as her rock, an immovable force of strength, foundation, and love. I'd like her to say that I tried to make her laugh every day. I hope she'll say that I took the edge off of her sharp corners, that even when I failed, I didn't give up.

I want her to remember the beach in Bermuda, the gondola ride in Venice, and the crazy friendships we've made on all of our trips. I hope she'll feel proud of the way we shared chores, wrestled and tickled our kids, and prayed for them daily. I hope she'll be able to say that I tried to do little things every day to care for her and to put her first.

I know I will say that I grew to become a better man because of her—emotionally, physically, and spiritually.

Go ahead and write down how you want you and your marriage to be remembered by your spouse, by your friends, by your children and grandchildren, and by all the people you've invested in. Now work backward and start to live it out—quarter by quarter.

The Abrahamic Covenant: A Blessing That Will Multiply

The Abrahamic covenant is a powerful example of legacy. By faith and relationship with God, Abram and his wife, Sarai, overcame incredible odds to build a rich legacy. The book of Genesis records the promise of blessing:

> The LORD had said to Abram, "Go from your country, your people and your father's household to the land I will show you.
>
> "I will make you into a great nation,
> and I will bless you;
> I will make your name great,
> and you will be a blessing.
> I will bless those who bless you,
> and whoever curses you I will curse;
> and all peoples on earth
> will be blessed through you."
>
> *Genesis 12:1–3*

God repeats the blessing later in Genesis: "I will surely bless you and make your descendants as numerous as the stars in the sky and as the sand on the seashore" (Genesis 22:17).

Abram was given a legacy vision from God. One minor detail: he received the vision about children at seventy-five years of age! But that didn't stop Abram and Sarai from living out their faith. In fact, God gave them new names—Abraham ("father of many") and Sarah ("princess")—before the promise was fulfilled because of their faith in action. It took another twenty-five years before their son Isaac was born. Abraham was one hundred years old!

Isaac grew up to be a great man in his own right. In Israel's drought and depression, Isaac was the one who began to dig again the wells that helped bring sustenance to the people. Isaac had a son named Jacob. Jacob started to go off course in the wrong direction, but he wrestled with God to receive a blessing from Him. Jacob had twelve children who became the twelve tribes of Israel. All of Israel's future real estate, jobs, and duties were destined through Jacob's seed. One of his sons, Joseph, would save a nation through his prophecy and persistence.

The seed of Abraham continued to multiply and to bless. Eventually, through the same family tree, Moses was born and would lead Israel out of 430 years of Egyptian captivity. David, a grandson x 13 of Abraham, became the king of Israel, and he led them into an amazing season of prosperity. Solomon came next and built the temple so the nation's people could consecrate themselves to God. Years after, the Israelites found themselves in exile again, and Zerubbabel, another descendant of Abraham, led Israel back into blessing and rebuilt the temple. The line went on and on, seeing the Lord's favor and blessing over a nation.

It continued until a descendant of Abraham named Mary was chosen to give birth to a son named Jesus. Jesus, the Savior, would offer blessing to all of humanity.

When you trace the line of Abraham and Sarah, you get a new understanding of how God can multiply the legacy of one's life and faith. When God said, "I will make you into a great nation, and I will bless you; I will make your name great, and you will be a blessing," He was giving a blessing of legacy—a blessing that would multiply and compound.

A Legacy Moment

Our bedtime tradition with the kids includes a story and a prayer. When Ella was younger, she always wanted to hear the story of her grandpa. Her grandpa, my father, left an indelible legacy. He founded Calvary Church in Naperville, Illinois, and pastored it for thirty years. The church now has nearly ten thousand people in attendance. Thousands have been baptized there. It has invested millions of dollars into local and international mission efforts. My dad was a giant of a man, physically and spiritually. When he was fifty-five years old and in the prime of his ministry, he died suddenly of a heart attack while at breakfast with a man he was discipling. It was a devastating loss to our family, but his legacy did not die with his body.

Each night at bedtime, Ella, my six-year old daughter, would ask me to tell her about Grandpa.

I'd say, "Ella, you never got to meet your grandpa, but he was a very good man. Do you know what people called him?"

She would respond, "Passor Bob."

"That's right, Ella. Thousands of people loved and cared about Pastor Bob, and he loved and cared for thousands of people. He was a really big man. Do you know that he had *huge* hands? His hands were large and thick. Your grandpa used to pray for people, and when he did, he'd take his big hand and put it on their heads, like this, and he would pray for them."

Each night, I'd place my hand on Ella's head and pray for her. I prayed the Lord's favor and blessing and passion, and that He would raise her up to be a leader in her generation. Amazingly, it was the only part of her day when she'd actually sit still! I don't know if it's because of the prayer or because she thought it was weird that I put my hand on her head, but it worked!

I prayed for her this way every night, but one night, the weight of his absence overcame me. I sat on the bed a bit despondent. I was filled with a great sadness, wishing my dad could have prayed over and into my daughter.

As I prayed over my little girl, God prompted this thought: *Your dad is praying for her—right now, through you. His legacy and his prayers live on through you.*

The thought caught me in such a way that I began to cry. I didn't just tear up, but I began to cry out loud. It wasn't movie crying, where you still look good, but the ugly kind, where your face starts contorting and people have to look away. Ella saw me and initially thought I was laughing, so she started giggling. After a second, she paused, sensing something was off. She had never seen her daddy cry.

She said, "Daddy, are you okay?"

I didn't want my little girl to see fear or weakness in her dad, her protector. But I asked the Lord to make it a teaching moment.

I said, "You've never seen this, but Daddy can get emotional when thinking about how much he and Mommy love our family. I was thinking about how much I loved your grandpa. I was thinking about how much I love you. I just wish you both could have met. But then I realized that what was given to me, I actually get to give to you."

It was a legacy moment. I realized that if I live a faithful life and have a faith-filled marriage, the blessings of God won't stop after I do. The blessings of my grandparents are still going. They're still going for my dad and mom. They're still going for Abraham and Sarah. As philanthropist Stanley Tam says, "God can't reward Abraham yet because his seed is still multiplying."[13]

When the storms of life come crashing down on you, it's hard to remember that God's blessings are still going. When you're warring, when you're disconnected, when you're off-balance, it's hard to see the greater story God is writing. It's important that you don't give up. My uncle Betta Mengistu used to say, "Whenever you have a setback, don't take a step back, because God has already prepared your comeback." We are believing for a blessing over your marriage today as you step out in faith to live out the legacy He has designed for you.

The psalmist encourages us with these words: "We will tell the next generation the praiseworthy deeds of the LORD, his power, and the wonders he has done" (Psalm 78:4).

Our Prayer for You: One Unbroken Circle

JOEL *&* **NINA**

O n the day that Honi the circle maker drew a circle in the dirt and stepped inside, he dropped to his knees, lifted his hands, and said, "Lord of the universe, I swear before Your great name that I will not move from this circle until You have shown mercy upon Your children."[1]

Honi's prayer was resolute. He was unwavering. His prayer was clear and specific. Honi's prayer has been called the prayer that saved a generation. Mark Batterson wrote in *The Circle Maker,* "The legend of Honi the circle maker stands forever as a testament to the power of a single prayer to change the course of history."[2]

It has been our prayer that God will strengthen your marriage through the circles you've read about in this book. We have prayed that He will give you a Holy Spirit–inspired vision. We have prayed that He will redeem your conflicts and restore you after storms. That He will stir up innovation and creativity within your marriage and grant you a renewed commitment to love. We believe that your prayers over your marriage or over a marriage close to you can change the course of history.

As is often the case when one responds in obedience to something the Lord prompts them to do, we have felt an increased burden for marriages during our writing of this book. During the months of writing, we've seen an abundance of challenges in marriages. We have seen couples who are broken and couples who are breaking up. We've seen young people getting married for the wrong reason and singles choosing not to get married for the wrong reasons. We have spent time on the couch with aspiring couples and time on our knees interceding in prayer for separating spouses.

However, we've also seen couples step out in boldness and achieve dreams together. We have seen a couple who had divorced find healing and get remarried. We have seen couples confront the trials in their marriage and through faith and persistence find new levels of love. While marriages seem to face more challenges than ever before, we have more hope than ever because of these testimonies.

We affirm the reality of the challenges in your marriage. But we want you to feel overwhelming hope in the midst of those challenges. Don't be dismayed. Don't be discouraged. Don't be defeated. When Jesus said, "Peace I leave with you" (John 14:27), He was speaking in the middle of conflict, tension, and turmoil that would continue. Jesus was speaking to the inside position of our hearts and minds as much as to the outside condition of our circumstances. Prayer doesn't allow us to remain sedentary in our situation. It pushes us to humble ourselves, to face our own weaknesses, to grow, and to put faith in the God who is able.

It has been our most consistent prayer that God will renew a commitment to prayer in your marriage. We've been petitioning the Lord to stir up a prayer revival in marriages! Throughout this book, we've included prompts for prayer and action. If you stopped to pray through each one, you have prayed twenty-six prayers for your marriage over the course of your reading. Those are words that have not fallen silent before the Lord. He hears them and responds to them.

We encourage you to go back and review some of the prayers you've prayed. Review some of your notes or journal entries. What are you asking of the Lord? What vision are you hoping He reveals? What conflict are you asking Him to overcome? What miracle are you trusting Him for?

Commit to pray with boldness and perseverance. Speak your prayers out loud to the Lord every morning when you awake and every night before you fall asleep. Choose a verse of Scripture and claim it over your marriage.

As we were challenged in *The Circle Maker*, "There is nothing God loves more than keeping promises, answering prayers, performing miracles, and fulfilling dreams . . . You are only one prayer away from a dream fulfilled, a promise kept, or a miracle performed."[3] We are believing that God can do something new in you and your spouse.

Of course, the purpose of prayer is not to get what we want

from God for our marriage. Its purpose is to commune with God and gain His heart for our marriage. God's desired result of prayer is not changing your spouse as much as it is changing you.

As you begin this prayer journey, receive this prayer of blessing over your marriage as you seek God's hand on your relationship. Allow us to close this book by praying a blessing over you.

Marriage is God's idea. He desires to answer the prayers for your marriage and your future, far beyond what you could ask or imagine.

From this day forward, may you be joined in mind and heart. May God reveal His purpose for your marriage and unify you in vision.

As you remember the original places of your love, may He remind of what brought you together.

May you rekindle your romance and continue to enjoy each other even beyond the way you did when you first fell in love.

May God grant you sensitivity in conflict and revelation about the true source of distance in your marriage. May you grow each day in understanding and compassion.

When frustration, difficulties, and fear assail your relationship, may God grant you the clarity to focus on what is right between you, not just the part that seems wrong.

May your lives be rich in friendship with others who support and counsel you. May you be open to invite others to speak truth and encouragement into your marriage.

May any pain or difficulty you face be something that strengthens rather than divides your marriage.

May you treat your marriage as sacred and honor it by living with integrity and commitment to one another.

May God grant you the faith to remain committed to a future together, even when the future seems uncertain.

Joined together in one unbroken circle, may God bless you and keep you always.

Acknowledgments

To Mark and Lora, who saw this book in us before we saw it ourselves. Doing life and ministry alongside you is one of the great joys of our lives.

To our children, Ella, Zeke, and Renzi, who endured the long hours of writing. Your patience and encouragement helped us achieve a dream. Our love and commitment to each other is a legacy we desire to leave to you.

To our parents, Karen and Bob, Kim and Bill, Mark and Sherry, thank you for loving us so completely. So much of who we are is because of your commitment and support.

To our extended family, who makes every memory sweeter. We are so grateful that when we married each other, we got you too.

To those who gave us the privilege of sharing their stories as a testimony of God's work in marriage, your vulnerability made us brave to share our own story—Amy and Adam, Heather and Nathan, Kristen and Jesse, Chris and Kathryn, Dave and Kate, Dick and Ruth, Doug and Kate, Dan and Tiffani, Julie and Michael.

To the friends and family who offered consistent words of encouragement and prayers through this process and believed for the work God wants to do in marriages—Mike and Robin, Dick and Ruth, JD and Melissa, Eugenia, Doug and Kate, Amy, Kerley, Paul and Colleen, Jim and Christy, Brandon and Kristina, Jenilee.

To our agent, Esther, for believing we had something to share with couples.

To our editors, Stephanie, John, and Dirk, and our publishing and marketing teams for your gracious support and diligent work. You are a valuable part of the work God will do in marriages through this book.

Notes

Foreword

1. Mark Batterson, *Praying Circles around Your Children* (Grand Rapids: Zondervan, 2012), 11.

Introduction: Circling Marriage

1. Mark Batterson, *The Circle Maker: Praying Circles around Your Biggest Dreams and Greatest Fears*, rev. ed. (Grand Rapids: Zondervan, 2011), 11–13.
2. Batterson, *Circle Maker*, 7.

Chapter 1: Vision Circle

1. Nick Greene, "Apollo 13: A Mission in Trouble," November 3, 2017, www.thoughtco.com/apollo-13-a-mission-in-trouble-3073470.
2. Visit www.bittersweetcreative.com to learn more.
3. Visit www.dcdreamcenter.com to learn more.
4. Mark Batterson, *Soulprint: Discovering Your Divine Destiny* (Colorado Springs: Multnomah, 2011), 2.
5. Rabbi Maurice Lamm, "Marriage and Community," www.myjewishlearning.com/article/marriage-community.
6. Lamm, "Marriage and Community."
7. Lamm, "Marriage and Community."
8. Lamm, "Marriage and Community."
9. Quoted in Society for Personality and Social Psychology, "How

We Form Habits, Change Existing Ones," *Science Daily*, August 8, 2014, www.sciencedaily.com/releases/2014/08/140808111931.htm.

Chapter 2: War Circle

1. See Gabrielle Frank, "What American Marriages Are Really Like in 2017," *Today*, June 26, 2017, www.today.com/health/what-it-s-be-married-2017-t112961.
2. Quoted in John Gottman, "The Truth about Expectations in Relationships," January 30, 2018, www.gottman.com/blog/truth-expectations-relationships.
3. H. Norman Wright, "How to Build an Enduring Marriage," July 3, 2010, www.youtube.com/watch?v=HH0pC2yTkdQ.
4. Dr. Terri L. Orbuch, *5 Simple Steps to Take Your Marriage from Good to Great*, rev. ed. (2009; repr., Austin, TX: River Grove, 2015), 76.
5. Emerson Eggerichs, *Love and Respect: The Love She Most Desires, the Respect He Desperately Needs* (Nashville: Nelson, 2004). 49.
6. A. Pearce Higgins, *The Hague Peace Conferences* (Cambridge: Cambridge University Press, 1909), 346.
7. R. A. Torrey, *How to Succeed in the Christian Life* (New York: Revell, 1906), 76.
8. Mark Batterson, *The Circle Maker*, rev. ed. (2011; repr., Grand Rapids: Zondervan, 2016), 23.
9. Batterson, *Circle Maker*, 23–24.

Chapter 3: Romance Circle

1. See Dina Kudasheva, "Chemistry of Love," Atomic Scale Design Network, http://asdn.net/asdn/chemistry/chemistry_of_love.php.
2. See Helen E. Fisher, Arthur Aron, and Lucy L. Brown, "Romantic Love: A Mammalian Brain System for Mate Choice," *Philosophical Transactions of the Royal Society B Biological Sciences* 361 (January 2007): 2173–86, www.researchgate.net/publication/6678968_Romantic_love_A_mammalian_brain_system_for_mate_choice.
3. Helen Fisher, *Why We Love: The Nature and Chemistry of Romantic Love* (New York: Holt, 2004), 182–83.

4. See Inna Schneiderman et al., "Oxytocin during the Initial Stages of Romantic Attachment: Relations to Couples' Interactive Reciprocity," *Psychoneuroendocrinology* 37, no. 8 (August 2012): 1277–85, www.ncbi.nlm.nih.gov/pmc/articles/PMC3936960/.

5. See Bianca P. Acevedo et al., "Neural Correlates of Long-Term Intense Romantic Love," *Social Cognitive and Affective Neuroscience* 7, no. 2 (February 2012): 145–59.

6. Sheila Wray Gregoire, *31 Days to Great Sex: Love, Friendship, Fun* (Winnipeg, MB: Word Alive, 2013), 39.

7. Gregoire, *31 Days to Great Sex*, 39.

8. See Arthur Aron et al., "The Experimental Generation of Interpersonal Closeness: A Procedure and Some Preliminary Findings," *Personality and Social Psychology Bulletin* 23 (1997): 363–77.

9. Michele Weiner-Davis, "The Unspoken Truth about a Sex-Starved Marriage," Huffpost, May 7, 2014, www.huffingtonpost.com/michele -weinerdavis/the-unspoken-truth-about-_1_b_5276291.html.

10. Gregoire, *31 Days to Great Sex*, 78–79.

11. See Gregoire, *31 Days to Great Sex*, 20.

12. See Jennifer P. Schneider and Burton H. Schneider, "Couple Recovery from Sexual Addiction/Coaddiction: Results of a Survey of 88 Marriages," *Sexual Addiction & Compulsivity* 3, no. 2 (1996): 111–26.

13. Helen E. Fisher et al., "Intense, Passionate, Romantic Love: A Natural Addiction? How the Fields That Investigate Romance and Substance Abuse Can Inform Each Other," *Frontiers in Psychology* 7 (May 2016), 687.

14. Gary D. Chapman, *The Five Love Languages: The Secret to Love That Lasts*, rev. ed. (1992; repr., Chicago: Northfield, 2015).

15. Quoted in Alice Calaprice and Trevor Lipscombe, *Albert Einstein: A Biography* (Westport, CT: Greenwood, 2005), 5.

16. See Marcus Buckingham and Donald O. Clifton, *Now, Discover Your Strengths* (New York: Free Press, 2001).

17. John Maxwell, *Talent Is Never Enough: Discover the Choices That Will Take You beyond Your Talent* (Nashville: Nelson, 2007), 184.

18. See Chapman, *Five Love Languages*, 173.

Chapter 4: Dance Circle

1. Quoted in Richard Corliss, "That Old Feeling: A Stellar Astaire," *Time*, June 22, 2002, http://content.time.com/time/arts/article/0,8599,265339,00.html.
2. Michelle N. Shiota and Robert W. Levenson, "Birds of a Feather Don't Always Fly Farthest: Similarity in Big Five Personality Predicts More Negative Marital Satisfaction Trajectories in Long-Term Marriages," *Psychology and Aging* 22, no. 4 (January 2008): 666–75.
3. Quoted in John Maxwell, *Becoming a Person of Influence: How to Positively Impact the Lives of Others* (Nashville: Nelson, 1997), 130.

Chapter 5: Support Circle

1. See Bruce Y. Lee, "Cigna Finds More Evidence of Loneliness in America," *Forbes*, May 1, 2018, www.forbes.com/sites/brucelee/2018/05/01/here-is-more-evidence-that-americans-are-lonely-and-what-should-be-done/#121c1ca3194f.
2. Shane Hipps, *Flickering Pixels: How Technology Shapes Your Faith* (Grand Rapids: Zondervan, 2009), 113.
3. Hipps, *Flickering Pixels*, 114.
4. Naomi Gerstel and Natalia Sarkisian, "Marriage Reduces Social Ties," Council on Contemporary Families, January 1, 2007, https://contemporaryfamilies.org/marriage-reduces-social-ties.
5. Tara Parker-Pope, *For Better: How the Surprising Science of Happy Couples Can Help Your Marriage Succeed* (New York: Penguin, 2010), 278.
6. Rose McDermott, James H. Fowler, and Nicholas A. Christakis, "Breaking Up Is Hard to Do, Unless Everyone Else Is Doing It Too: Social Network Effects on Divorce in a Longitudinal Sample," *Social Forces* 92, no. 2 (December 1, 2013): 491–519.
7. Shasta Nelson, *Friendships Don't Just Happen! The Guide to Creating a Meaningful Circle of Girlfriends* (Nashville: Turner, 2013).
8. Cited in Jen Hatmaker, "Girlfriends Can Save the World," For the Love podcast, episode 3, http://jenhatmaker.com/episode-03-shasta-nelson.htm.

9. C. S. Lewis, *The Four Loves* (1960: repr., New York: Harcourt, Brace, 1991), 78.

10. Stephanie Coontz, "How to Stay Married," *Times of London*, November 30, 2006, www.stephaniecoontz.com/articles/article34.htm.

11. Gary Chapman, *The Four Seasons of Marriage: Secrets to a Lasting Marriage* (Carol Stream, IL: Tyndale, 2012), 19.

12. Chapman, *Four Seasons of Marriage*, 45.

13. Henri Nouwen, *The Inner Voice of Love: A Journey Through Anguish to Freedom* (New York: Random House, 2010), 25.

14. Thomas Watson, *A Divine Cordial; the Saint's Spiritual Delight; the Holy Eucharist; and Other Treatises* (London: Religious Tract Society, 1846), 22.

Chapter 6: Storm Circle

1. Cited in Tom Watkins, "Problems with Haiti Building Standards Outlined," *CNN*, January 13, 2010, www.cnn.com/2010/WORLD/americas/01/13/haiti.construction/index.html.

2. Cited in Cynthia Bourgeault, "Centering Prayer: The Method," Center for Action and Contemplation, February 13, 2017, https://cac.org/the-method-2017-02-13.

3. John M. Gottman and Nan Silver, *The Seven Principles for Making Marriage Work: A Practical Guide from the Country's Foremost Relationship Expert* (New York: Crown, 1999), 61–78; see H. Wallace Goddard, "Commitment in Healthy Relationships," *Forum for Family and Consumer Issues* 12, no. 1, https://projects.ncsu.edu/ffci/publications/2007/v12-n1-2007-spring/godddard/fa-10-goddard.php.

4. Quoted in Stuart Wolpert, "Here Is What Real Commitment to Your Marriage Means," UCLA Newsroom, February 1, 2012, http://newsroom.ucla.edu/releases/here-is-what-real-commitment-to-228064.

5. Sara Miller Llana, "Mexico's 'Temporary' Marriages: Till Death—or Two Years—Do Us Part," *Christian Science Monitor*, November 1, 2011, www.csmonitor.com/World/Americas/2011/1101/Mexico-s-temporary-marriages-till-death-or-two-years-do-us-part.

Chapter 7: Legacy Circle

1. Story paraphrased from Miriam P. Feinberg and Rena Rotenberg, *Lively Legends-Jewish Values* (Denver, CO: A.R.E. Publishing, 1993), 47–58; see "Honi Ha-Me'agel Sleeps for Seventy Years," Religious Action Center of Reform Judaism, https://rac.org/program-bank-story-about-honi.

2. Mark Batterson, *Draw the Circle: The 40-Day Prayer Challenge* (Grand Rapids: Zondervan, 2012), 30.

3. Edward Hickman, ed., *The Works of Jonathan Edwards* (London: William Ball, 1839), 1:56.

4. Tim Clinton, *Before a Bad Goodbye: How to Turn Your Marriage Around* (Nashville: Word, 1999), 46.

5. Paraphrased from "Alfred Nobel Created the Nobel Prize as a False Obituary Declared Him 'The Merchant of Death,'" Vintage News, October 14, 2016, www.thevintagenews.com/2016/10/14/alfred-nobel-created-the-nobel-prize-as-a-false-obituary-declared-him-the-merchant-of-death.

6. Allan Luks, "Health Benefits of Kindness," *Pathways to Family Wellness* 19 (Fall 2008), http://pathwaystofamilywellness.org/Inspirational/health-benefits-of-kindness.html.

7. Danica Collins, "The Act of Kindness and Its Positive Health Benefits," Underground Health Reporter, October 18, 2014, http://undergroundhealthreporter.com/act-of-kindness.

8. Emily Esfahani Smith, *The Power of Meaning: Finding Fulfillment in a World Obsessed with Happiness* (New York: Broadway Books, 2017), 10.

9. See Smith, *Power of Meaning*, 14–15.

10. Smith, *Power of Meaning*, 14.

11. "22 Quotes from Andy Stanley at Exponential 2018," Injoy Stewardship Solutions, February 28, 2018, www.injoystewardship.com/articles/22-quotes-from-andy-stanley-at-exponential-2018.

12. "Tiny Sacrifices," Preaching Today, www.preachingtoday.com/illustrations/1997/june/714.html.

13. A comment Stanley Tam made over dinner after speaking at National Community Church.

Afterword: Our Prayer for You: One Unbroken Circle

1. Mark Batterson, *The Circle Maker*, rev. ed. (2011; repr., Grand Rapids: Zondervan, 2016), 12.
2. Batterson, *Circle Maker*, 13.
3. Batterson, *Circle Maker*, 15.

The Circle Maker

Praying Circles Around Your Biggest Dreams and Greatest Fears

Mark Batterson

New York Times *bestseller!*
More than one million copies sold!

According to Pastor Mark Batterson in this expanded edition of *The Circle Maker*, "Drawing prayer circles around our dreams isn't just a mechanism whereby we accomplish great things for God. It's a mechanism whereby God accomplishes great things in us."

Do you ever sense that there's far more to prayer than what you're experiencing?

It's time you learned from the legend of Honi the Circle Maker—a man bold enough to draw a circle in the sand and not budge from inside it until God answered his impossible prayer for his people.

What impossibly big dream is God calling you to draw a prayer circle around?

Sharing inspiring stories from his own experiences as a circle maker, Mark Batterson will help you uncover your heart's deepest desires and God-given dreams and unleash them through the kind of audacious prayer that God delights to answer.

This expanded edition of *The Circle Maker* also includes Batterson's newest insights on how God answers prayer, along with stories that add convincing proof to the reality that God is able to do immeasurably more than all we could ask or imagine.

Now also available—*The Circle Maker* Spanish edition, prayer journal, student and kids editions, parent editions, small group studies, video curriculum, and more.

Available in stores and online!

Draw the Circle

The 40 Day Prayer Challenge

Mark Batterson

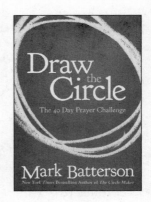

Do you pray as often and as boldly as you want to? There is a way to experience a deeper, more passionate, persistent, and intimate prayer life.

In this forty-day devotional, Mark Batterson applies the principles of his *New York Times* bestselling book *The Circle Maker* to teach you a new way to pray. As thousands of readers quickly became many tens of thousands, true stories of miraculous and inspiring answers to prayer began to pour in. These testimonies will light your faith on fire and help you pray with even more boldness.

In *Draw the Circle*, through forty true, faith-building stories of God's answers to prayers, daily Scriptures, and prayer prompts, Batterson inspires you to pray and keep praying like never before.

Begin a lifetime of watching God work. Believe in the God who can do all things. Experience the power of bold prayer and even bolder faith in *Draw the Circle*.

Available in stores and online!

Draw the Circle Prayer Journal

A 40-Day Experiment

Mark Batterson

Experience a deeper, more passionate, and intimate prayer life. If you press into God's presence like never before, you will experience God like never before.

Drawn from bestselling books by Mark Batterson, this bullet journal will guide you into more intentional prayers, with forty days of Scripture verses, inspirational readings, prayer prompts, and beautifully designed spreads for journaling.

Designed for reflective writers, Bible journalers, and prayer list-makers, everyone who adventures outside the line will find the freedom to customize these dotted pages to your unique prayer style.

The *Draw the Circle Prayer Journal* will become your written record for dreaming big, praying hard, thinking long ... and seeing God's answers.

Available in stores and online!

The Circle Maker for Kids

One Prayer Can Change Everything

Mark Batterson; illustrated by Antonio Javier Caparo

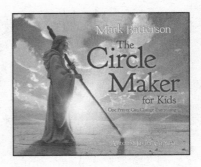

A terrible drought had hit the land. Gardens died; rivers ran dry; the Israelites had one last hope: Honi the rainmaker. So they called on him to pray, and Honi did something strange—something bold. Would God send rain and save the people? Basing this story on his adult bestseller *The Circle Maker*, Mark Batterson shares the ancient Jewish legend of Honi the rainmaker with children to teach them about the power of prayer.

The Circle Maker, Student Edition

Dream Big, Pray Hard, Think Long

Mark Batterson with Parker Batterson

In this student adaptation of *The Circle Maker*, Pastor Mark Batterson uses the true legend of Honi, a first-century Jewish sage whose bold prayer saved a generation, to unpack what powerful prayer can mean in your life. Drawing inspiration from his experiences as a circle maker, as well as sharing stories of young people who have experienced God's blessings, Batterson explores how to approach God by drawing prayer circles around your dreams, your problems, and, most importantly, God's promises. In the process, you'll discover a simple yet life-changing truth: God honors bold prayers and bold prayers honor God.

And you're never too young for God to use you for amazing things.

Praying Circles around Your Children

Mark Batterson

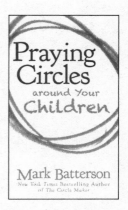

In this 112-page booklet, Mark Batterson shares a perfect blend of biblical yet practical advice that will revolutionize your prayer life by giving you a new vocabulary and a new methodology. You'll see how prayer is your secret weapon. Through stories of parents just like you, Batterson shares five prayer circles that will not only help you pray for your kids, but also pray through your kids.

Batterson teaches about how to create prayer lists unique to your family, claim God-inspired promises for your children, turn your family circle into a prayer circle, and discover your child's life themes. And he not only tells you how, he illustrates why.

As Batterson says, "I realize that not everyone inherited a prayer legacy like I did, but you can leave a legacy for generations to come. Your prayers have the power to shape the destiny of your children and your children's children. It's time to start circling."

Available in stores and online!